BRIGHT IDEAS

Starting points

Written by William Edmonds

Published by Scholastic Publications Ltd,
Villiers House,
Clarendon Avenue,
Leamington Spa,
Warwickshire CV32 5PR

© 1994 Scholastic Publications
Text © 1994 William Edmonds

Author William Edmonds
Editor Noel Pritchard
Assistant Editor Kate Banham
Designers Joy White and Tracey Ramsey
Illustrations by Pauline King
Cover design by Lynda Murray
Cover photograph by Martyn Chillmaid
Designed using Aldus Pagemaker
Processed by Pages Bureau, Leamington Spa
Artwork by Lynda Murray
Printed in Great Britain by Clays Ltd, St Ives plc

British Library Cataloguing-in-Publication Data
A catalogue record for this book is available from the British Library.

ISBN 0-590-53155-7

The right of William Edmonds to be identified as the Author of this work has been asserted by him in accordance with the Copyright, Designs and Patent Act 1988.

All rights reserved. This book is sold subject to the condition that it shall not, by way of trade or otherwise, be lent, hired out or otherwise circulated without the publisher's prior consent in any form of binding or cover other than that in which it is published and without a similar condition, including this condition, being imposed upon the subsequent purchaser.

No part of this publication may be reproduced, stored in a retrieval system, or transmitted, in any form or by any means, electronic, mechanical, photocopying, recording or otherwise, without the prior permission of the publisher except where photocopying for educational purposes within a school or other educational establishment is expressly permitted in the text.

Contents

4 INTRODUCTION

6 NEW YEARS AND TERMS

SETTLING IN ACTIVITIES 8
Welcome   8
Who are we?   9
Dear Miss   10
New sensations   11
Look at us now!   12
Facts and figures   13
Any questions?   14
Looking ahead   15
Creating an image   15
Classroom calendars   16
Any suggestions?   17
Holiday curiosities   18
A first book   19
Background display   20

LANGUAGE ACTIVITIES 21
Learning names   21
First day back   22
First verse   23
Words of introduction   24
Model reading   25
Book choice   25
Holiday snaps   26
Holiday highlights   27
Jolly holidays   28

MATHEMATICAL ACTIVITIES 29
Counting up   29
Measuring up   30
Calculating along   31
Weighing in   32
Rounding up   33
Initial estimates   33
Shaping up   34
Squaring up   35
Projections   36

NEW SEASON ACTIVITIES 37
Seasonal greetings   37
Summing up summer   38
Signs of autumn   39
Welcoming the Jewish New Year – Rosh Hashanah   40

Welcoming the Hindu New Year – Diwali 41
Welcoming the Muslim New Year – Eid-ul-Fitr 42
Welcoming January – Hogmanay 43
Welcoming the Chinese New Year 44
New Year resolve 45
New Year honours 45
Years in orbit 46
Winter nights 47
Wake up! It's spring 48
Spring sowing and growing 49

50 NEW DAYS

MONDAY MORNING ACTIVITIES 51
Telling time 51
Journals with a difference 52
Chart the week 53
Monday news-sheet 54
Monday moods 54

LANGUAGE ACTIVITIES 55
Listings 55
Letter of the day 56
Bright and early 56
Spelling teases 57
Substitution word play 57
Test reading 58
Writing in style 58
Word of the day 59
Alphabet ordering 60
Dictionary search 60
Story starts 61
Read, quote, illustrate 61

MATHEMATICAL ACTIVITIES 62
Grouping 62
Shape seeking 63
Number of the day 63
Equal areas 64
Lots and lots 64
Grid patterns 65
Detecting number patterns 66
Morning surveys 67
Shape shading – fractions 68
Long lines 69
Coded messages 70
Problem challenges 71

72 NEW STARTS THROUGH THE DAY

SPECIAL ASSIGNMENTS 74
Make a magic castle 74
Sort six counters 75
Draw and count 76
Invent a new toy or game 77
Spell the magic 78
Researching parrots 79
Picture to shape 80
Puzzle with cubes 81
Weigh a box of goods 82
Imagine you're a mouse 83
Observe and draw 84
Test with a magnet 85
Calculate number rows 86
Measure the distance 87
Question and quiz 88
Process a story 89
Listen in 90
Report on the weather 91
Two minute tasks 92
Ten minute tasks 92

COMING TOGETHER AGAIN 93
Secret numbers 93
Secret operations 94
Secret words 95
Hot seat 96
Solve the problem 97
Co-ordinating 98
Telling stories 99
Brainstorms 100
Golden silence 101

102 REPRODUCIBLE MATERIAL

Introduction

How do we make sure that each new school year or new term has a flying start? What are good ways of starting each day and how do we keep on coming up with good ideas for making new starts many times through the day?

These are the challenges that all primary teachers know only too well. The opportunities for making fresh starts in primary schools are immense, but these are equalled by the demands on teachers to come up with bright new initiatives. Here, then, is a collection of starting-point ideas designed to provide a support for all those countless initiative-demanding situations.

'Getting it right from the start' places a heavy onus on teachers, as we know how easily children can be directed along blind alleys of confusion or misapprehension. On the other hand, a stimulating and appropriate start can set minds alight and engage long-lasting enthusiasm. Sound beginnings are the first requirements for creating solid foundations. The activities set out in this book are therefore especially tailored for the sharp end of educational practice, where first impressions and first encounters are all important.

The book has three chapters which relate directly to the challenges set out at the beginning. In each chapter there is a strong emphasis on getting to grips with basic skills, especially relating to language and mathematics, but in ways that make these skills relevant and appealing. In the first two chapters, concerned with starting school years (and terms) and with how to begin each day, there is an emphasis on the children working together towards common objectives and with the aim of establishing a strong class coherence. In the third chapter, concerned with making 'new starts through the day', there is a section of 'special assignments' with ideas for more independent work by individuals and small groups. Finally there is a selection of 'coming together again' activities on which the class and teacher can work actively as a whole.

The level of each activity is indicated by an 'age range' section but these are only rough guidelines and teachers may select activities appropriate to the needs of their children. By the same token teachers can decide on the best group size with which to carry out each activity – individuals, in pairs, small groups or the whole class.

ACTIVITY SELECTION

Although the activities in each section apply to three rather different situations, they can be used with a considerable degree of flexibility and teachers will be able to adapt the ideas to fit the particular needs and circumstances of their classes. Special extra resources are rarely needed, ensuring that most 'starts' can be made in straightforward and uncomplicated ways.

Many of the activities can either be adopted as self-sufficient one-off exercises, brief warm-up or fill-in activities, taking anything from just a few minutes to up to half an hour. Or, if desired, they can be used as introductions to more lengthy and developed work. Of course, as all teachers know, there is a considerable degree of unpredictability about what will catch on and then really take off so there are also plenty of suggestions for renewed and fresh starts.

Now it's time to start making use of this book. Good luck! Good beginnings!

New years and terms

Starting a new school year – a new class and a new teacher meeting each other for the first time, and all somewhat apprehensive after a long holiday break – is a critical time. From the very first day and the very first lesson, important patterns of conduct are set and key impressions are created. On the one hand, there has to be a gentle, general easing in for everyone. On the other, it is good to get things organised right from the outset. It is gratifying and rewarding for all concerned if the new class rapidly achieves for itself a new and distinctive identity. Meanwhile, many introductions have to be made: of names, of basic procedures, of the classroom layout and resources available, and of how to start new books and use new materials.

Starting a new term part-way through a school year also presents a special challenge. It is a natural time for reappraising and modifying classroom management and general curriculum planning. It may coincide with New Year resolutions and the heralding of a new season or seasonal time. The beginning of any new term also allows you to take advantage of the special stimulation provided by a variety of holiday experiences. It can be a good time for appraisal activities to show new stages of personal or class development. Certain activities, therefore, might lend themselves to being repeated or adapted at the beginning of each term. But, perhaps most significantly, the beginning of each new term is a time for fresh expectations when the sense of anticipation can seem more immediate.

Settling in activities

Welcome

Objective
To promote a welcoming ambience in a new class by making appropriate notices for the classroom entrance.

Age range
Five to nine.

What you need
Pencils, paper, felt-tipped pens, crayons, scissors, coloured backing paper, adhesive.

What to do
Start with a general discussion about the idea of making the classroom a friendly and welcoming place to enter. Ask the children to suggest practical things that might be done about this, especially ways of greeting people as they come into the room. Steer the discussion particularly towards considering what kind of notice or notices would be most appropriate to put on the door. Maybe a single sizeable notice will be thought to be most suitable. In that case, the children could each, or in pairs, help to make and decorate one letter for a slogan. For example:

> WELCOME TO THE WONDERFUL WORLD OF CLASS 2

Give the children paper cut to a regular size and show them how to make their letters to fit the height of the paper. The letter can first be drawn with a light pencil line and then its thickness can be created by drawing another line around this. The inside of the letters can then be coloured, in designs created by the children. After they have been coloured the letters will need to be cut out and placed on a larger background paper, ready to be stuck down. Children who finish first can do any extra letters that may be needed or go on to produce further decorative motifs to add to the poster.

Alternatively, individual or small groups of children could make their own welcoming notices, each one perhaps drawing attention to a different aspect of the class – a general welcome followed by a more specific one.

> Welcome to Class J2. Enjoy a browse among our books!

> Welcome to Class J2. Visit our Exciting Science Corner!

> Welcome to Class J2. Meet our Gorgeous Gerbil, Jim!

Follow-up
Display small portraits and character sketches of all the members of the class under a sign saying, for example, 'Welcome to Class 2. Meet its Cheerful Children!'

Who are we?

Objective
To make vivid spoken and written self-introductions with the aid of questioning and questionnaires.

Age range
Seven to eleven.

What you need
Copies of the questionnaire on photocopiable page 103, examples of biographical blurbs (as on the backs of some books), pencils, paper.

What to do
Firstly, tell the children that you are looking forward to getting to know them and finding out what is special about each one of them. Then engage in a discussion aimed at discovering individual special interests and personal backgrounds. Slightly quirky questions like the following might be helpful in drawing out more interesting responses:
- Who has a special interest that they are crazy about?
- Who has a funny pet?
- Who has a bossy brother or sister and what kinds of things do they have to put up with from them?
- What's your favourite time of day, music, food, football team, place?
- Who can play a musical instrument or do clever tricks?

When every child has been drawn into making some contribution, tell the class that you would like them each to introduce themselves to you more fully with the aid of a questionnaire. Ask them either to write down answers on the questionnaire itself or to use the list of questions as a guide to producing a piece of free writing with a title like 'Who am I?'

Another way to approach this activity is to start by looking at a few examples of authors' biographical blurbs sometimes found on the backs or insides of books. After a discussion about how adequate these are, the children can set out to emulate and improve on the general idea by composing their own self-promotional blurbs.

Follow-up
- Put all the written introductions together to make 'An introduction to the class' book or wall display.
- Draw portraits or self-portraits to accompany the introductions.

Dear Miss

Objective
To use a letter format to make personal introductions. This activity can take a bit of time and effort but it is one way of helping to establish a personal rapport with each child right from the start.

Age range
Seven to eleven.

What you need
Pencils, pens and paper.

What to do
A good way to start this activity is for the teacher to write and duplicate a general letter which can then be addressed personally to each child. It could be something like the example on the right.
 A copy of such a letter, inside an envelope, could be waiting for each child on their desk when they arrive first thing in the morning. Or, alternatively, a copy could be attached inside the front cover of each child's new writing book. Give a short explanation about the letters – perhaps including a short discussion about how it is sometimes easier to say things in the semi-privacy of a letter than it is by speaking more publicly – and then invite the children to make their replies.

Follow-up
- You could make short individual acknowledgements and replies to the children's letters. The correspondence could well continue for some time.
- The letters and replies could form the basis for a special 'letters' book.

Dear ...

Welcome back to school and to my new class!
I hope you had a good holiday. Did you have any good adventures? Did anything exciting or special happen to you? Or did you have any scary moments? Please tell me! I would love to hear any good stories of what you have been up to recently. I had a good time myself, except I got seasick and nearly fell off the boat going to the Isle of Wight.

Doesn't it feel funny to be back at school again after the long holiday? I can tell you that it is a strange feeling for teachers too. I wonder what is the best thing about it for you or what are the not-so-good things? Can you tell me what you enjoy most at school and what are your least favourite things, or the things that you are not so good at? Have you any special interests which you are mad about or keen to learn more about?

I look forward to reading a letter from you with answers to some of my questions. Please tell me anything you would like me to know about yourself, your family, your pets and your interests. If you have any questions, I will be pleased to try to answer them too.

Best wishes for an excellent new school year!

New sensations

Objective
To make full use of the senses in describing the experience of arriving in a new classroom.

Age range
Five to nine.

What you need
Paper and pencils.

What to do
Introduce a short class discussion about the senses and how they can be more acute when you are doing something or going somewhere for the first time. Then briskly ask the children what new things they are noticing in the classroom with their eyes, their ears, their noses and their hands, bottoms and/or feet. When it comes to smell it may well be sufficient to identify things that have distinctive smells rather than trying to describe the smells themselves. After the children have named a full range of new sensations ask them to make their own 'new sensations' lists.

Look at us now!

Objective
To make verbal and visual self-portraits as a record of a particular day.

Age range
Five to nine.

What you need
Drawing and writing paper, pens or pencils, felt-tipped pens or crayons.

What to do
Explain to the children that this time of year, that is, at the beginning of the school year, is one of those times that they are quite likely to look back upon in months or possibly years to come. Tell them that they are going to make personal portraits so that they will all have a record for the future of what today was like for them. Divide the class into pairs and ask each child to draw a portrait of their partner. If there is a large mirror available some of them can draw self-portraits. Their portraits should show main facial features and clothes.

Afterwards, or at a slightly later time, ask the children to *write* a short self-portrait to go with their drawing. You could give them a specimen such as the one below.

> My name is ....
>
> I'm .... years old
>
> I'm .... m .... cm tall
>
> I'm wearing ....
>
> I'm .... (where are you?)
>
> I'm busy .... (what are you doing?)
>
> It's a .... (what kind of day is it?)
>
> I'm feeling ....
>
> I just want to say ....

Follow-up
- Mount the drawn and written portraits to make a classroom display or book.
- Repeat the exercise at the beginning of each term and note any changes.

Facts and figures

Objective
To demonstrate the combined knowledge, experience, skills, interests, loyalties and attributes of the new class.

Age range
Seven to eleven.

What you need
Photocopiable pages 104–5, calculators, weighing scales, tape measures (or a height measurer), pencils, paper.

What to do
First of all, work out with the children what is the approximate total age of the whole class (the average age times the number of pupils). Express amazement at the total and what it represents in terms of the amount of different individual experiences and of different things learned – far more than that of any one adult, even you, their teacher. Go on to discuss what other collective statistics might be worked out about all the class: totals of height, weight, languages spoken, countries visited, particular talents and so on. When the children begin to appreciate fully the scale of what they have collectively rather than individually, tell them that they are going to do a survey among themselves to find out and publicise the extent of their 'greatness'.

Give each child a copy of the questionnaire on pages 104–5 and ask them to complete it. Then different groups within the class can be allocated different sections of the questionnaire to collate (the sections having been completed on small separate pieces of paper or else subsequently cut out from a single sheet. The totals can be pooled to produce a final 'PR' newsletter to be given to visitors and perhaps read out in a school assembly.

Any questions?

Objective
To develop a sense of curiosity by stimulating children to ask questions about what they want to know.

Age range
Five to eleven.

What you need
Paper, pencils.

What to do
This is an activity that can be adapted to fit a wide age range and therefore a wide range of interests and preoccupations. At any age the exercise will be more productive if some guidance is given about the range of questions that could be asked on particular themes, for example: school, old times, birth, animals, how things began, God, other places, Space, your future, the future of the world, funny worries or concerns and so on.

An initial discussion where you can encourage the children to ask their own questions will be helpful, but the relative confidentiality of individual writing should produce a wide range of interesting results. In this case, the teacher will have to use discretion about how openly the questions are subsequently collated and dealt with.

To make the collation easier each question should be written down on a separate piece of paper and initialled by the writer. It is also a good idea to give the whole exercise a title to focus on, such as: 'Wondering', '101 questions about this and that', 'What I/we want to know about...'

Follow-up
- Make a book or booklets of all the questions unanswered or answered.
- Collate the questions and compile a class question list. This could be put on display and completed gradually as follow-up work and research is carried out during the following weeks.
- Invite relevant experts to visit your class and answer particular questions.

Looking ahead

Age range
Five to eleven.

What you need
Pencils and paper.

What to do
This is an activity that can be modified greatly in detail and sophistication according to the age of the children. In general you should begin with a talk about how a new term or new school year is a time for wondering what will happen, looking forward to new things and setting sights on fresh ambitions both for the near and distant future.

Younger children could be asked simply to say what they think they would like to do, or be, when they are grown up. Discuss and compare different ideas and ask the children to draw pictures of themselves in such a future time with simple accompanying captions.

Older children could be asked to plot their future lives in more detail. This could focus on what they aim to achieve and do in the following hours, days and weeks, and maybe also on how they see themselves in successive years or stages of their whole lives. Such work could be written up schematically as 'maps of the future', which might include other worldwide events as well as personal ones.

Creating an image

Objective
To promote a collective identity for the class or groups within the class by designing logos or emblems.

Age range
Seven to eleven.

What you need
Examples of printed logos, badges or emblems, a variety of publicity literature where logos can be found, felt-tipped pens and/or crayons, A4 paper.

What to do
After looking at – and maybe also searching for – some examples of different kinds of logos, discuss with the children which ones they like most and which they think are most effective in conveying an intended message. Steer the discussion towards asking what kind of sign would be appropriate for this class or each class group. Then ask the children individually, or in pairs, to draft their own idea for such a sign. When this is done, all the draft ideas can be put on temporary display and the class can vote to see which is the most popular. The design can then be worked on and copied, and so be used thereafter for classroom or group publicity.

Classroom calendars

Objective
To plan ahead for the new term by making calendars.

Age range
Seven to eleven.

What you need
A4 paper printed in a standard format (as shown in the illustration), pencils, crayons or felt-tipped pens, a copy of the main school calendar and of a basic year calendar.

What to do
Discuss which months lie ahead in the current term and what events may be happening during these months:
- birthdays;
- parents' evenings;
- sports fixtures;
- poetry weeks;
- religious festivals;
- class assemblies;
- outings and so on.

List the dozen or so weeks of the term on the board and together work out the date on which each of these weeks begins. Indicate too on this master list the principal events that came up in the discussion, and maybe give each week a special title – John's (birthday) week, Guy Fawkes' week, Harvest Festival week. Then assign particular weeks to small groups of children and ask them to make up an appropriate calendar page on the prepared sheets, each one with a suitable picture in the main frame. If each child completes one page it should be possible to compile two or three class calendars, one of which could be donated to the school office.

Follow-up
- Ask the children to mark off the days on the calendar as they pass and also mark in any other significant events as they occur or are planned.
- Ask the children to make their own one- or two-page calendars for the whole term.

Any suggestions?

Objective
To promote children's involvement in classroom management by inviting them to make suggestions.

Age range
Five to eleven.

What you need
A shoebox-sized cardboard box, slips of paper, pencils.

What to do
Tell the children that the classroom is going to have a suggestion box in which they can put written suggestions about the general organisation of the classroom or school. Discuss the range of possible subjects for their suggestions. These may include some or all of the following: the arrangement of furniture in the classroom, the decoration of the walls, dealing with litter and tidiness, time-saving ideas, story requests, class rules, visitors they might like to invite and so on.

Assign two or three children to make and decorate a suggestion box and ask the others individually, or in pairs, to write a suggestion to be put into this box. When this is done, set a time to discuss the suggestions and decide what to do about them.

Follow-up
Keep the suggestion box in the classroom for continual use (including by visitors) through the year.

Holiday curiosities

Objective
To create situations in which the children introduce themselves to the class by talking about special objects found during the holidays.

Age range
Five to nine.

What you need
A reserve assortment of special objects similar to those mentioned below.

What to do
Tell the children that you want them each to try to bring into school something curious that they may have found (*not* bought) during the holiday. This item could be anything – a curious coin, unusual-shaped stone, piece of metal or wood, fossil, shell, feather or anything that has caught their attention and made them look twice. Tell them also that such items may often suggest a story, of a mysterious past history, for example. suggest to the children that they should tell or make up a story to go with each object that they bring. In case some children do not bring in any such object, it is a good idea if you have a small reserve of such curiosities in the classroom for them to choose from and make stories about.

Once the objects have been brought in, they can be laid out and labelled in a special exhibition space. The class can then have a number of sessions when individual or pairs of children present and tell stories about their curiosities.

Follow-up
- Ask the children to write short illustrated stories to make a collected exhibition guide.
- Present the exhibition of curiosities to other audiences – other classes, a school assembly or parents.

A first book

Objective
To make and compile a *First book* to include all the first bits of work undertaken in the first week of the year.

Age range
Five to eleven.

What you need
Pieces of coloured paper for covers, cut to double the standard writing paper size; regular sized pieces of writing and drawing paper, pencils, pens, felt-tipped pens, a stapler.

What to do
On the first day or two of term give each child a piece of coloured paper to act as a cover folder for the pieces of work done during the first week. Tell the children that at the end of the week all their work will be combined together to make a book. A simple way of doing this is to staple single sheets together inside the folding cover but for this purpose, the children should be told to take care always to keep a clear ruler-width margin on each piece of paper and, if reverse sides of the pages are used, also to keep a margin on the right-hand side. At an appropriate stage ask the children to make cover designs, perhaps making use of simple line patterns (waves, zigzags and so on). When finally preparing the collections of work for stapling the children should be asked to insert an introductory contents page and to put a small personal blurb on the back cover.

Background display

Objective
To carry out introductory colouring and patterning exercises to make backgrounds for classroom display boards.

Age range
Five to eleven.

What you need
Paints, thick brushes, long strips of paper (approximately 10cm x 60cm) for border patterns, large rectangular pieces of paper according to display board areas, scrap paper, newspaper for lining tables as the painting may go over the edges of the paper.

What to do
There are two parts to this activity which can be undertaken in varying degrees of sophistication according to the age of the children. These can either be carried out by the whole class on two separate occasions or by smaller groups during one session.

The first part involves making colour-wash background papers to line display boards. This provides an opportunity for exploring the idea of differing colour intensities and how they can be produced by diluting a single colour with varying quantities of water. It is best to decide upon a single colour for the background of each board and then experiment with scrap paper to find which paint and water mixture gives a satisfying effect and easy application without making obvious brush marks. Older children can try making striped papers with varying intensities of a single colour.

The second part of the activity involves making border patterns to frame the edges of the display boards. For the sake of consistency and the matching together of the patterns, the children should be directed or asked to agree upon a particular style – say a zigzag pattern, wavy or straight stripes with a limited colour range. The patterns could be done in paints or crayons, or a combination of both, but if a large number of strips are needed, paints will produce quicker results.

Language activities

Learning names

Objective
To aid recognition of children's names and to draw attention to common spelling features.

Age range
Five to seven.

What you need
Name cards for all the children in the class, a display board, Blu-Tack, felt-tipped pens.

What to do
This activity is best carried out as a short exercise repeated at the beginning of the day. Ask the children to find their name card first thing each morning and place it in front of them. To start with, the children can be asked to show the names with a particular initial letter. All the names starting with that letter can then be displayed together on the board. Once the children are familiar with initial letters they can be asked to show names with other letter features, such as ones containing a certain vowel or certain combinations of letters. This can extend to looking for short words inside names (*cat*, *the*, *her*, *in* in *Catherine* or *an*, *ant*, *on* in *Anthony*).

First day back

Objective
To make and collect observations about the sensation of a first day back at school and then use these to make poems.

Age range
Seven to eleven.

What you need
A chalkboard, chalk, paper, pencils.

What to do
Firstly, ask the children to consider what is new for them on this first day back. Ask them such questions as:
- What's new for you about today?
- What's new and different about this classroom compared to the one you were in previously?
- What new people have you met (names of staff, children and so on?)
- Have you noticed any new smells, sounds or sights?
- What new clothes are you/anybody else wearing?
- Are there any new things that anybody has brought to school or noticed in school?

Now continue the discussion by asking what kind of feelings the children have about their first day back:
- Can anyone describe the strangeness that they are feeling today?
- What's good about being back at school?
- What's not so good about being back at school?
- What things are you looking forward to doing again, or for the first time?
- What kind of things are you worried about having to do?
- Can you think of one word to sum up what it is like for you to be back at school?

During this discussion it is a good idea to write some of the key words and ideas that come up on the board. When a full range of ideas and issues have been raised the children can be asked to list their own individual impressions of this first day back to make a poem. You could provide a model framework for this, such as:

First day back

New .....

New .....

New .....

New .....

New .....

Feeling .....

Feeling .....

Wondering whether ....

Wishing ....

Looking forward to ....

Hoping that ....

First day back.

Isn't it ......!

First verse

Objective
To memorise a poem and be able to recognise it as one of the first things learned on the first day.

Age range
Seven to eleven.

What you need
A short memorable poem which is likely to stimulate a lively response from the children (for example 'The Spangled Pandemonium'* by Palmer Brown – shown opposite – or 'The Jolly Hunter'** by Charles Causley) written up on the board, pencils, paper, and possibly coloured pens/pencils for drawing illustrations.

What to do
Tell the children that they are going to learn something new and special for their first day back at school – they are going to learn a poem and fix it in their memories. A very effective way of doing this is first to read the poem through with the children two or three times directly from the board. Then ask them to recite it again after you have rubbed out the last word of each line. Work through verse by verse in this way, and gradually rub out more and more of the words, eventually leaving just the first few words of each line as a prompt.

To give them a break from the repeated reciting the children can be asked to write down the list of prompt words and also, perhaps to draw and colour an illustration for the poem.

If possible, practise reciting the poem again before the end of the day and add a little more dramatic effect each time.

Follow-up
- Give a simple performance of reciting the poem in a school assembly.
- Make beautiful illustrated copies of the poem as a handwriting exercise for a wall display or for the start of compiling poetry anthologies.

Amazing Monsters – Verses to Thrill and Chill edited by Robert Fisher (Faber & Faber, 1982).
**In several anthologies, including *Strictly Private – An Anthology of Poetry* chosen by Roger McGough (Puffin Books, 1981).

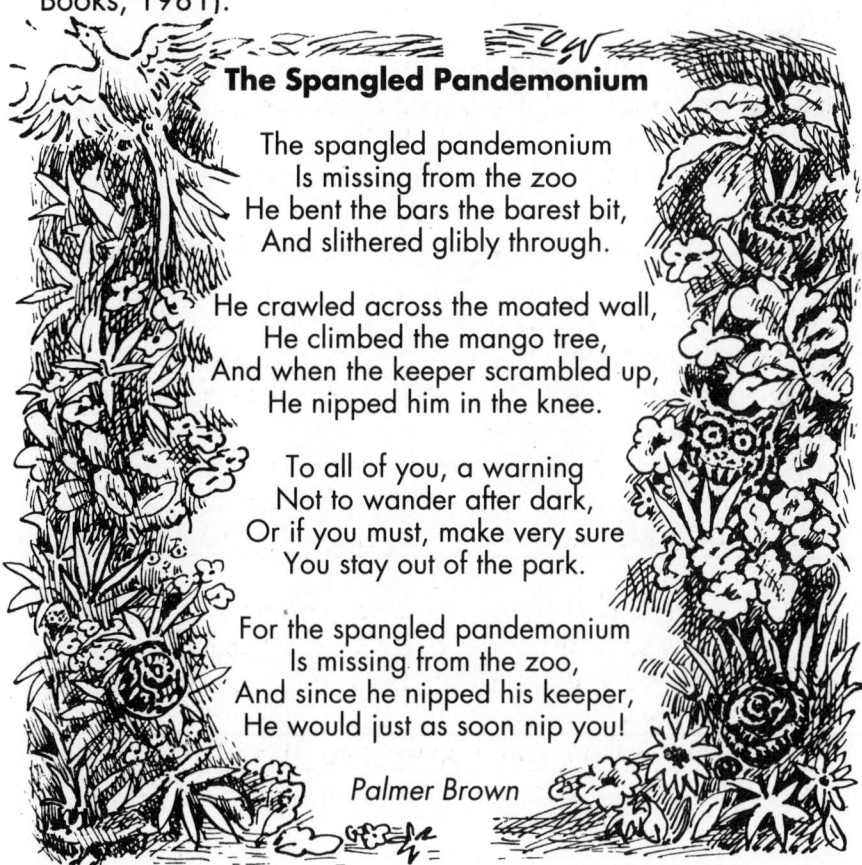

The Spangled Pandemonium

The spangled pandemonium
Is missing from the zoo
He bent the bars the barest bit,
And slithered glibly through.

He crawled across the moated wall,
He climbed the mango tree,
And when the keeper scrambled up,
He nipped him in the knee.

To all of you, a warning
Not to wander after dark,
Or if you must, make very sure
You stay out of the park.

For the spangled pandemonium
Is missing from the zoo,
And since he nipped his keeper,
He would just as soon nip you!

Palmer Brown

Words of introduction

Objective
To introduce a major topic for study by creating familiarity through key vocabulary associated with that topic.

Age range
Seven to eleven.

What you need
A variety of dictionaries, encyclopaedias and relevant information books, a list of words associated with a chosen topic written on the chalkboard or on a poster (for example: How the solar system began – *beginning, dust, gas, swirling, burning, fire, sun, planets, meteorites, asteroids, satellites, orbiting*).

What to do
Tell the children that they are going to start learning about a new topic and that on the board are some important words which sum up what the subject is all about. Follow this by giving a brief summary of the subject matter and drawing their attention to the words you have listed. Explain that knowing the right words – the jargon – goes a long way to knowing about any subject and that you now want them to find out more about these words so that they will be able to explain them well, easily recognise them and spell them correctly.

It may be best if different groups of children research different groups of words, finding, if possible, alternative dictionary definitions or alternative reference book explanations. The results of research can then be pooled and put on display.

Follow-up
- Ask the children to test themselves on the spelling and explanation of all these words and, maybe, prepare for a general class test or presentation.
- Make topic dictionaries.
- Look for words that have similar roots: *meteorite, meteors, meteoric, meteorology*.

Model reading

Objective
To read a story to a class as a fully shared reading experience and to model reading techniques.

Age range
Five to seven.

What you need
A good picture book with large print and a memorable and succinct text which also has a predictable refrain, pieces of card, pens/pencils.

What to do
Gather the children together closely in front of you. Tell them that you are going to read a story and then afterwards you are going to read it again with their help. Point at the words while you read.

On the second reading, wait at certain predictable points (such as final words of sentences) and ask the children to read these parts for you. Write these words on pieces of card and congratulate the children on being able to read them. Point out the differences between these words and try to convince the children that they also can easily distinguish them.

Follow-up
- Use the same technique to draw attention to short full sentences in the story.
- Draw more attention to the composition of some of the words, especially to initial letters or words with common phonemes.
- Set the children the ambition of being able to read the whole story each for themselves.

Book choice

Objective
To consider and apply criteria for choosing suitable books to read.

Age range
Seven to eleven.

What you need
A reasonable classroom library of fiction and non-fiction books, card, pens/pencils.

What to do
Ask the children for different things to look for when choosing a good book to read and write their ideas on the board. These might include names of favourite authors, books of a particular size, attractive covers, appealing illustrations, books with lots of text or books with lots of pictures, books that are easy/not too easy to read, stories about children, adults or animals, books on particular topics and so on. When a reasonable list of criteria has been made, ask the children each to say and maybe vote upon their top reason for choosing a book.

Now tell them each to find a book according to their top choice category and to read it during their silent reading time. When they finish reading this book, and if they still agree that it fits their chosen category, ask them to put it on a display table with a label identifying its category, and naming and dating by whom and when it was read.

Adventure story about children

Read by ....
Date ...

Holiday snaps

Objective
To represent special moments of recent holiday experiences with photo-like pictures and succinct captions.

Age range
Five to seven.

What you need
Some 'holiday snaps' (the teacher's or a child's), pieces of photo-sized thin white card, coloured pencils or thin felt-tipped pens, strips of paper for writing captions.

What to do
Start by looking at just a few examples of holiday photographs and asking the children to suggest captions – either based on memories of the actual occasions represented or, if the pictures are unfamiliar, by 'making them up'. To make the captions more interesting the children should be encouraged to mention not only who, or what, and where the photograph is of, but also what the characters might have been thinking at the moment the photograph was taken, what they were doing just previously or what they were about to do. Encourage the children to appreciate that the photographs only show what happens in a fraction of a second and that they can be thought of as 'captured moments' which usually tell or hint at a much longer story – just like a video still. Once the children begin to appreciate this idea ask them to recall special 'fraction-of-a-second' moments of their own holidays – moments when they had a sudden surprise, experienced something especially delightful, a triumph, an accident, a shock or a fright – moments which tell of much longer stories.

When all the children have thought of special holiday moments they can then be asked to draw and colour their own small 'snap-shot' pictures of these occasions. Ask them to make sure that all the background parts of the pictures are coloured in to make them as photo-like as possible. After completing the pictures, the children can write captions which not only tell about the moment but also give some idea of the background story.

Follow-up
• Make a classroom wall display of all the 'holiday snaps' and captions.
• Make a presentation of the 'holiday snaps' to another audience – visitors, parents or another class – showing the pictures and giving succinct commentaries.
• Write longer stories based on the pictures.
• Ask the children each to bring in a real holiday snap or postcard and then make captions and/or commentaries.

Holiday highlights

Objective
To develop children's expressive and imaginative abilities through drama relating to recent holiday experiences.

Age range
Seven to nine.

What you need
Use of an empty space, such as the school hall.

What to do
Start with a general discussion involving all the children about what they think are the different components that make up a holiday experience. These may best be considered in some kind of chronological sequence, such as:
- packing and getting ready;
- setting off;
- first arriving;
- coping with strange foods;
- a picnic;
- a typical day;
- an unusual adventure;
- a day when everything goes wrong;
- meeting someone unusual – making new friends;
- coping with boring or tedious times like long car journeys;
- coming home again and noticing changes since you have been away.

Divide the children into groups of four to six then assign one part of a holiday story to each group and ask them to prepare and practise a short enactment of this. When enough time has been allowed for this, the groups can each perform their piece for the rest of the class. The whole exercise may then be repeated again with the assigning of more parts or variations of them.

Follow-up
- The members of each group can write a script or a dialogue for their part of the story.
- The acting can be polished to make a presentation to a wider audience, such as a school assembly.
- Write stories using the ideas above as chapter headings.

Jolly holidays

Objective
To invite the children to compare their recent holidays with a traditional fictional holiday adventure story and go on to write stories which slightly send up their own holiday and the fictional one.

Age range
Nine to eleven.

What you need
Examples of holiday adventure children's books (such as Enid Blyton's *Famous Five* series and more recent ones like Norma Clarke's *Patrick in Person*, Faber & Faber 1991), writing paper/book, pens or pencils.

What to do
Read to the class an opening section of a typical holiday adventure book. After reading a page or two of this to give a general picture the teacher should then stop and ask the children how they think the story might continue. Can they also suggest what some of the later chapter headings might be and compare these with those in the book?

Ask them whether their own holidays were in any way like this then follow this by asking them to jot down a number of possible chapter headings and a title that they would use if they had to write a holiday story based on their own recent experiences. Emphasise that the story need only be roughly based on truth and that a degree of fictional licence is quite acceptable. Once the children have produced possible formats for such stories they could go on to write a sample chapter in full.

Follow-up
- Produce a whole holiday adventure book or series of books based on agreed characters and chapter titles/synopses and ask different children to write each of these chapters.
- Collect together a variety of books on this theme – with the assistance of a librarian, if possible. Encourage a general critical reading of these, or possibly a summarising and comparative analysis of their plots.

Mathematical activities

Counting up

Objective
To undertake a general inventory of classroom items and to represent effectively the quantities assessed.

Age range
Five to seven.

What you need
Pencils, felt-tipped pens, small and large pieces of paper, an assortment of classroom materials that the children can count.

What to do
Tell the children that together they are going to count up everything in the classroom. Suggest a few examples of objects that can be counted, like chairs, tables or pairs of scissors for instance, and ask them to make some other suggestions. The teacher should represent each potential item with a simple diagrammatic symbol down the side of a big sheet of paper as the beginnings of a large chart. Together the class can make a count of a couple of examples – say the number of boys and the number of girls – and the teacher can demonstrate how these can be represented by drawing simple diagram figures and a summary number.

Afterwards the children can work in groups of four to six to do their own counting of selected items, represent them and mark the appropriate number. Finally, the results can be put together on a big classroom chart.

Follow-up
Make subsequent regular recounts to keep track of the items through the term or year.

Measuring up

Objective
To make measurements and comparisons of personal and other heights in the classroom.

Age range
Five to nine.

What you need
Rulers, tape-measures, height measurer (not absolutely necessary), a large piece of paper (preferably with centimetre square markings), one-and-a-half metre (approx.) strips of paper marked off in centimetres, assorted pencils, adhesive.

What to do
Tell the children that they are going to measure their heights and the heights of other things in the classroom. Discuss first which things are taller than them and which are smaller.

In front of all the children, make or complete the making of a big measuring chart on the wall. The basis of this could be a succession of standard classroom rulers (30cm lengths) fixed in a vertical line alongside two metre rules. Show the children how they can now use this to find out and mark their heights and the heights of other classroom objects.

Make sure that they understand about measuring their heights from the same base (that is, without wearing shoes) and by holding a flat object like a book level with the top of the head. (If possible, this operation should be supervised by an older person.) Also explain and demonstrate to the children how they can make paper strips, numbered in centimetres, cut to the same length as their height and then attach these to the chart. The children can all be set to work numbering off the centimetres and naming and colouring these strips, while in small groups (four to six) they come to be measured for their heights, and then trim the lengths of their strips accordingly.

Those children who complete their own height strips before the others can go on to make strips to indicate the heights of different pieces of classroom furniture.

Follow-up
- Make new measurements later in the year and add to the strips on the chart.
- Make small height charts using A4-sized pieces of centimetre squared paper. Number the centimetres along the left-hand side of the paper and indicate (by drawing round the objects, maybe) the heights of different items of desk equipment – various pencils, crayons, erasers, scissors, adhesive pots/tubes and so on – making sure that their bases are all level with zero on the numbered edge.

Calculating along

Objective
To make and use counting strips or squares which serve as computer-like aids for introductory counting exercises.

Age range
Seven to nine.

What you need
Paper metre strips marked off in centimetres or squares of paper marked with 100 smaller squares, pencils, paper.

What to do
Explain to the children that they are going to make simple counting machines or 'computers' which they can then use to help with basic calculations. There are two ways of doing this.

The simpler form of 'computer' is a number strip. For this, the children simply write in the numbers from 1 to 100 on a long paper strip. To help avoid the odd error caused by missing or duplicating a number, it is a good idea first to mark and fold the paper off in sections of 'ten'. To help distinguish each group of ten, each successive fold or section of ten numbers could be lightly shaded in alternate colours. The completed strip can then be used as an aid for helping children with simple additions (counting on) and subtractions (counting back).

The slightly more elaborate form of 'computer' is the 100 number square. For this, the children write the numbers 1 to 100 on a square piece of paper, itself already marked into 100 squares, making sure that each horizontal line finishes with a tens number. Such squares can then be used to aid any calculations with addition and subtraction up to 100. Counting in tens can be done vertically and counting in single units horizontally.

Follow-up
- If the strip is marked off in centimetre intervals then it can also serve for linear measuring tasks.
- Make multiplication charts using 100 square (or more) sized paper, with rows of numbers progressing in ones, twos, threes and so on.

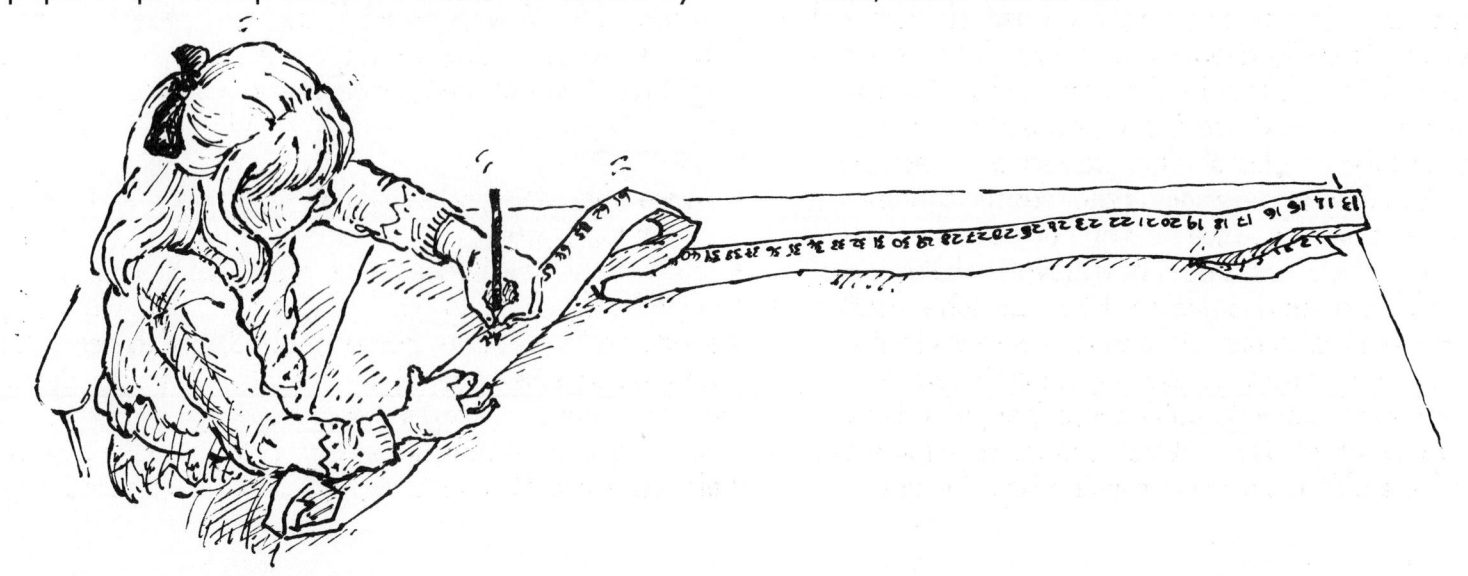

Weighing in

Objective
To assess the individual and total weights of the children, their school bags or their lunch boxes.

Age range
Five to eleven.

What you need
Weighing scales, pocket calculators, pencils, paper.

What to do
Talk to the children about what they bring to school, and comment jokingly that some of them might be staggering to school weighed down by things they are carrying, on top of the weight of their own body. Tell them that they are going to find out just how much is being carried. This can then be done either by each child measuring and recording their own weights or the weights of something they have brought to school, or else by taking average examples and multiplying up. (Sensitivity may be called for when dealing with children's personal body weight.) The totalling is probably best done with a calculator and the final results should be recorded on a wall chart.

To give some idea of what these measurements represent, the children should be asked to find other things in the classroom which have the same weight. For example, a bag of sand could be made up to the equivalent of an average body weight, and a pile of books could be made to equal the total weight of lunch boxes.

Follow-up
Assess the total weight of bodies at a school assembly, the total weight of food eaten at a school lunch and so on.

Rounding up

Objective
To practise rounding up prices or sums of money to the nearest 'whole' or more rounded figures.

Age range
Five to nine.

What you need
Pencils and paper.

What to do
Discuss with the children how shop prices are often marked just below rounded figures so as to give the impression that something is cheaper than it really is. Ask the children to give or look out for some examples. Then present the children with copies of a price list to be rounded up like the example below.

article	actual price	nearest whole price	saving
ice-cream	47p		
crisps	18p		
book	2.95		
shoes	19.95		

total savings =

What you could buy with this: ....

Follow-up
- Use this procedure with pages from actual catalogues.
- Adopt similar procedures for 'rounding down' or 'slashing' prices.

Initial estimates

Objective
To estimate quantities and then check how accurate you are.

Age range
Seven to eleven.

What you need
Jars containing various quantities of different small objects (buttons, counters, dried peas, small cubes and so on), pencils, paper.

What to do
Divide the children into groups of four to six and put a jar filled with a substantial quantity of small objects on each group table. Tell the children that you want each group to discuss how many small objects there are inside their jar and then for each person to write down their own estimate. When this is done they should empty their jars and count the contents – with each child or pair of children laying out and counting a separate smaller pile to be finally totalled together. Afterwards they can each see how close their initial estimates were and perhaps try again with a different jar of small objects.

Older children can be given more challenging tasks counting much larger quantities like grains of rice and sugar and finding other ways of assessing the quantities – by weighing, counting and multiplying small samples, for example.

Shaping up

Objective
To appreciate how regular straight-sided shapes can be put together to make further shapes including the extension of two dimensions into three dimensions.

Age group
Seven to eleven.

What you need
Templates of equilateral triangles, squares, pentagons and hexagons; drawing paper, thin card, adhesive, pencils.

What to do
There are two stages to this activity. They can be used according to what is appropriate to the development level of your children.

1. Two-dimensional combinations
Divide the class into at least four groups and give each group a number of templates of one of the regular shapes. Ask them to experiment with making their own arrangements of these shapes and then draw attention to the different patterns that are made or might be made. Such arrangements should include trying to make enlarged versions of their original shape and also placing shapes around the sides of a single shape. Examples of all the arrangements can then be displayed and compared. It is also a good idea to make more durable records of these patterns by drawing round the template arrangements.

2. Combining two-dimensional shapes into three dimensions
After carrying out the above, the children should be challenged to find out which of the template shapes can be combined to make 'nets' of solid three-dimensional shapes. Squares and equilateral triangles do so quite simply, pentagons will combine into dodecahedrons but hexagons by themselves will only combine as a flat grid pattern. Once this is understood the children can draw nets – with joining flaps – on thin card and make up some tetrahedrons, cubes and dodecahedrons. The latter, of course, is a much greater challenge appropriate for more able children.

Follow-up
- Investigate and tabulate characteristics of the solid shapes: numbers of faces, edges and corners for each shape or successive numbers of them.
- Combine regular solid shapes to make enlarged regular and irregular shapes (or speculate on this). For example, two tetrahedrons can be used to make a three-dimensional diamond shape.

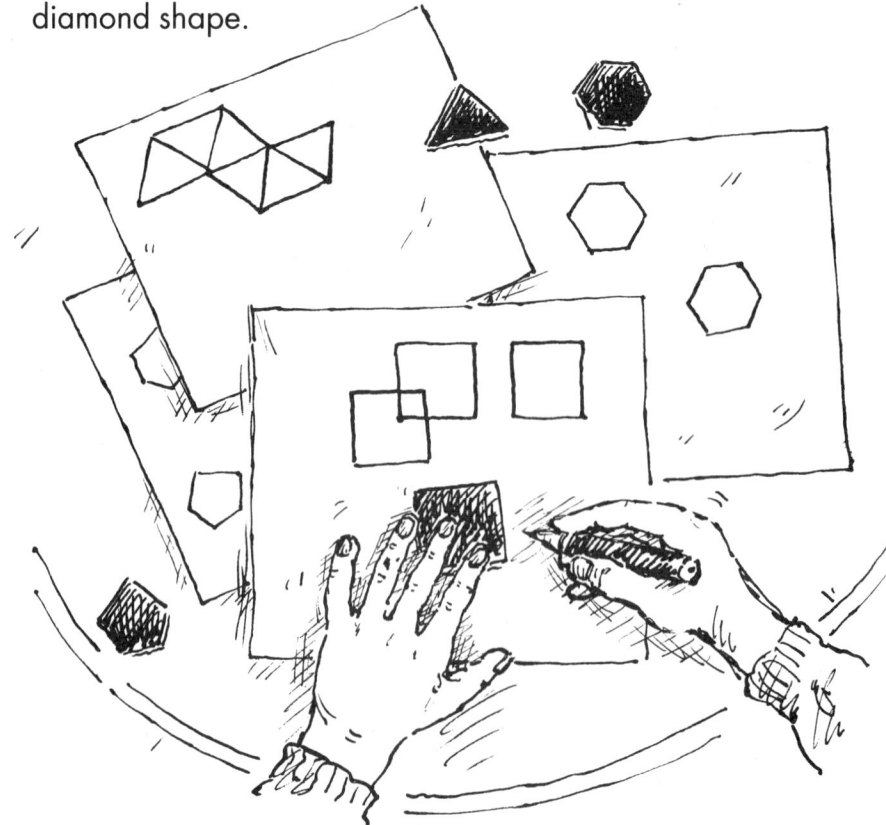

Squaring up

Objective
To focus on the concept of square numbers.

Age range
Nine to eleven.

What you need
Squared paper, a chalkboard, pocket calculators, pencils.

What to do
Write a few numbers on the board, including one or two square numbers (4, 9, 16 and so on) and challenge the children to say which of them could be called square numbers and why. Show how the numbers four and nine can be represented as larger squares made from smaller squares (two rows of two squares or three rows of three squares) as shown in Figure 1. Ask them to try to find out how further square numbers can be worked out, and also to say what rule they are using to make these numbers. Challenge the children to suggest a different rule or different ways of building up successive square numbers – for example, the rule of adding successive odd numbers (as if extending the square on two sides). See Figure 2.

Then ask the children to make and represent a sequence of square numbers up to a certain point (say 100). Following on from that they can perhaps be asked to find more square numbers with the help of pocket calculators.

Older children can be shown how to represent square numbers by inserting a small superscript figure two (x^2).

Follow-up
Cut out and arrange larger squares to make even larger squares and introduce and develop the concept of area.

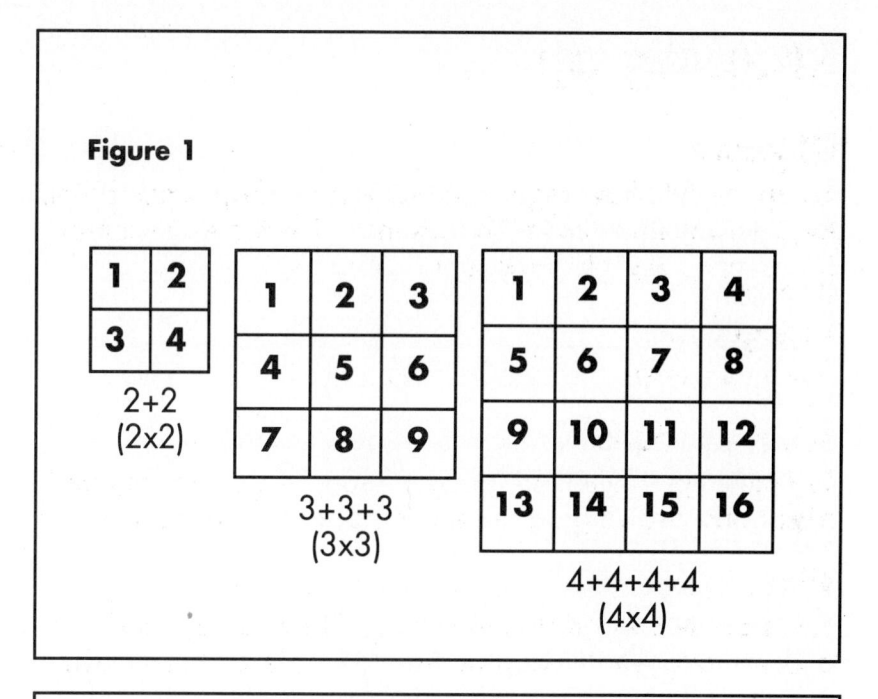

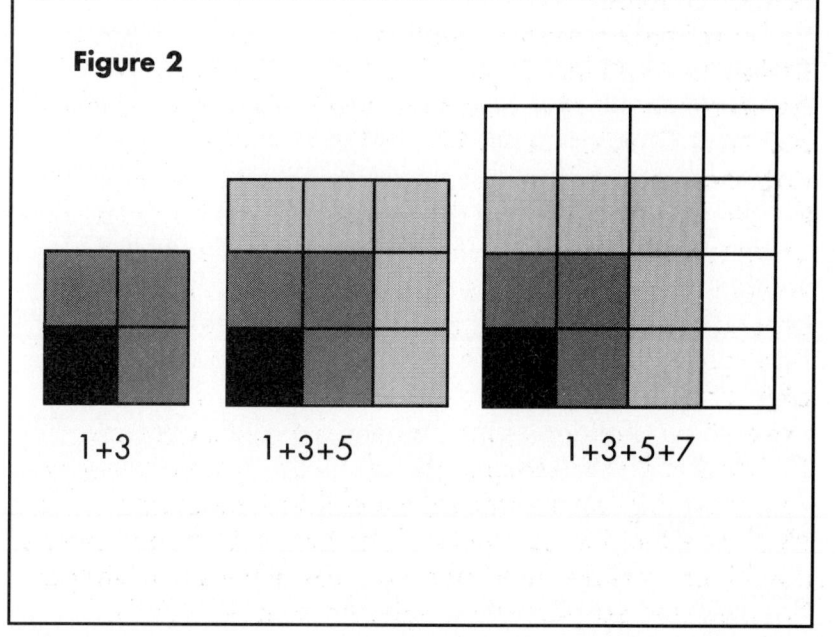

Figure 1

2+2
(2x2)

3+3+3
(3x3)

4+4+4+4
(4x4)

Figure 2

1+3

1+3+5

1+3+5+7

Projections

Objective
To make quantitative estimates of time and work involved in the forthcoming term or year.

Age range
Nine to eleven.

What you need
School calendars and timetables, pencils, paper, calculators.

What to do
Ask the children to make estimates for such questions as:
- How many school days are there this term?
- How many school hours are there?
- How many hours are scheduled for doing each of the major subjects like Mathematics, English and Science.
- How many pages or books will you read or write?
- How many kilometres will you walk to and from school?

After a variety of questions and estimates have been made, tell the children that they are going to make some precise projections along these lines.

As a start, it would be a good idea to work out the number of forthcoming school days together in consultation with a calendar. Then set a small number of projection tasks for all the children to work out individually, in pairs or in small groups. After completing the set tasks, the children could go on to make a few further projections about matters of their own choice.

Follow-up
- Present some of the gathered information in graph form.
- Extend the projections to include future school years.

New season activities

Seasonal greetings

Objective
To make greetings cards and decorations to welcome the coming of new seasons.

Age range
Five to nine.

What you need
Small pieces of card, drawing and collage materials, string, adhesive.

What to do
Tell the children, 'It's time to greet the coming of a new season.' Ask them what kinds of things they can look forward to with the approach of this season. If the new season is autumn, they may come up with such ideas as playing with conkers, kicking leaves, eating apples, planting bulbs, preparing for bonfire night, putting on warmer clothes, the beginning of the football season, watching new series of television programmes.

To help greet the season, suggest that the children make greetings cards with appropriate drawings or collages, and write greetings messages inside to particular friends or relatives.

For the classroom, simple decorations could be made with coloured images joined together on strings to go round the doorway or the windows.

Follow-up
Develop the theme with writing poems, composing songs and presenting a school assembly.

Summing up summer

Objective
To make recollections of 'summer days' as they draw to an end and represent these creatively in poetic writing.

Age range
Seven to eleven.

What you need
Pencils and paper.

What to do
Suggest to the children that as summer is coming to an end it is a good time to think back and sum up what it has been like. One way to start this is to ask the children to think of words to describe some of the different kinds of days that they can remember. They may need a little prompting to come up with a good variety of descriptions, such as hot, rain, cloudy, stormy, long, strange, brilliant, lazy, exciting, boring, happy, travelling, barbecue, party, festive and so on. The suggested words should be written on the board. Now with a few of the examples, ask the children to amplify what might be happening or what they might have been doing on such a day (swimming and eating ice cream on hot days, catching fish on exciting days, doing nothing very much on boring days and so on). Then the children can be invited to compose their own poems by listing and amplifying their own descriptions of summer days. You might also suggest that they decide on a particular formula to repeat:

> Long hot days when ...
>
> or Lovely hot days when ...
>
> or Horrible hot days when ...

Follow-up
- Older children, in particular, can be asked and helped to edit and redraft their first attempts to make more polished second versions.
- Produce paintings and drawings to illustrate particular kinds of days.
- Mime actions for the days and make a presentation of these.
- Alternatively, the same procedures could be applied to anticipating a forthcoming season as opposed to recollecting one.

Signs of autumn

Objective
To collect, observe and record scientific evidence indicative of this season.

Age range
Five to eleven.

What you need
Access to a park, garden or part of the countryside; copies of the observation chart on photocopiable page 106, pencils, notebooks, plastics bags, binoculars (optional), reference books.

What to do
Announce to the children that they are going to examine signs of autumn. This can either take the relatively simple form of a basic challenge to find and list such signs or else it can involve a more directed and detailed investigation.

In the first case, begin by issuing a challenge for the class to come up with a target number of 'signs' (say ten) that demonstrate the arrival of this season. Ask for first suggestions and show how these may fall into different categories, for example: weather conditions, sun positions, what's happening to leaves, flowers in bloom, fruits that can be gathered and animal activity, but insist that before any sign can be listed, evidence for it has to be provided.

Alerted in this way, the class – armed with pencils and notebooks, plastic bags for collecting and possibly binoculars – can make an excursion to a local park or part of the countryside and work in groups to see what evidence can be noted and collected. On return to the classroom each group of children should list and identify (with reference books, if necessary) their items of evidence, making sure that, as far as they know, their items are peculiar to autumn as opposed to any other season. When each group has finished sorting their own evidence the items can be listed in a collated form on a large class chart to see whether the target has been met.

Almost certainly there will be further signs to be noticed and these can be added in the course of the next few days, or possibly weeks, after more prompting, discussion and recording of evidence. As well as making a class list of signs the children can gradually add to their individual or group lists. Illustrations and labelled displays of the evidence will obviously also be worthwhile.

In the second case, present the children with an investigation chart (see photocopiable page 106) and, after some guidance, ask them to make specific observations and recordings at short regular intervals over a period of a month – or maybe over the whole of the first half term. At the end of this time ask them to make basic conclusions arising from their records.

Follow-up
Adapt and repeat the above procedures for signs of winter, spring or summer.

Welcoming the Jewish New Year – Rosh Hashanah

Objective
To celebrate Rosh Hashanah by sharing apples and tasting them with honey.

Age range
Five to eleven.

What you need
Apples, table knives, honey, paper napkins, a ram's horn or picture of one.

What to do
At the time of Rosh Hashanah (usually in September or early October) tell the children that they are going to hold a little celebration of a special day – the day that Jewish people celebrate as the beginning of their new religious year. Tell them that this day traditionally starts with the blowing of the *shofar*, a ram's horn, which calls the people to prayer. Explain how this is a day for being particularly in awe of God, the creation of the world and its abundance of fruits and foods. Tell them that the class can celebrate this day together in the traditional way by sharing and eating apples with a little bit of honey which is meant to represent the start of a fruitful new year.

Give each group of children an apple and ask them to find different ways of dividing their apples into equal parts, and so demonstrate a variety of fractions. The pieces of apple should then be shared and the children invited to dip them into honey before eating them.

NB Bear in mind the need for hygiene and any allergic reactions that may arise from eating these foods.

Welcoming the Hindu New Year – Diwali

Objective
To celebrate the Festival of Lights, Diwali (which immediately precedes the beginning of a Hindu and Sikh New Year), by making and displaying candles.

Age range
Five to eleven.

What you need
Materials for making model candles – cardboard tubes, coloured foil paper, sequins and other decorative material and/or material for making real candles – candle wax, coloured crayons, safe heating equipment, moulds; suitable recordings of Indian music, Indian sweets, Books of Indian stories, for example *The Story of Rama* (Kestrel Books).

What to do
Tell the children or ask Hindu and Sikh members of the class to help tell the story of Diwali – when Rama, the legendary god-king, and his wife Sita return to their kingdom after 14 years of exile and are guided by thousands of lights lit by the people. Tell them that they are going to make their own candles to celebrate Diwali and the coming of the Hindu and Sikh New Year. Younger children can then proceed to make model candles after you have demonstrated standard techniques. Older children may make real coloured candles, again following standard craft procedures.

Make a special display of the candles for the day of Diwali (in October or November) and hold a celebration by listening to appropriate music, tasting Indian sweetmeats and telling or acting out some of the classical Indian stories.

Follow-up
Tell the children that Diwali is also a time for stopping old quarrels and ask them to think about and demonstrate how they can do this themselves.

NB Bear in mind any food allergies children may have when eating Indian sweets and foods.

Welcoming the Muslim New Year – Eid-ul-Fitr

Objective
To celebrate Eid-ul-Fitr by making and displaying greetings cards.

Age range
Five to eleven.

What you need
Pictures of Islamic geometric patterns, schematic flowers and birds (as on Turkish carpets), new-moon crescents, mosque minarets (see reference books such as *The Muslim World* Richard Tames (Macdonald); thin card, coloured foil, adhesive, felt-tipped pens, scissors.

What to do
Tell the children or ask any Muslim members of class to help you tell the background story of Eid-ul-Fitr – the festival of fast-breaking – which comes at the end of the month of Ramadan during which Muslim people were instructed by the prophet Muhammad to fast during daylight. The date of Eid-ul-Fitr changes each calendar year because it follows lunar months, but it is always signalled by the first appearance of the new moon after Ramadan, and this heralds the beginning of a new Islamic year.

Tell and show the children how to make greetings cards for this occasion. Give them copies of the special greeting 'Eid Mubarak' in Urdu script (as shown below) to put on their cards and show them a range of Islamic designs (not figures) which they might also try to copy or adapt for their cards. Islamic script goes from right to left, so the cards should be made with the fold on the right-hand side.

During one of the three days of the festival hold a small celebration displaying the cards and tasting almond cakes and sugared almonds.

NB Bear in mind any food allergies children may have when tasting the cakes and sweets.

عید مبارک

Welcoming January – Hogmanay

Objective
To celebrate the beginning of January with special attention to the Roman god Janus and Scottish traditions.

Age range
Five to eleven.

What you need
Images of the double-faced Roman god Janus, (which can be found in books on time, such as the *Big Book of Time* W. Edmonds (Reader's Digest), large paper bags, felt-tipped pens, assorted decorative materials, adhesive, scissors, Scottish shortbread, a book of Scottish folk tales, recorded Scottish folk music.

What to do
Tell the children that they are going to make a special celebration for the beginning of the new calendar year and month. Tell them about Janus – the Roman god who had two faces, one looking forward to the future and one looking back to the past. Explain that the first month of the Roman calendar (our calendar, too) was named after him because he was the god of gates and doors and so of beginnings and openings.

Show the children how to make simple doubled-faced Janus masks with large paper bags or to make double-faced figures on pieces of card to hang up in the classroom.

Also tell them about Hogmanay, the celebration of the beginning of the calendar year in Scotland – a special time for dancing, drinking, eating treats like shortbread and welcoming strangers. Then hold a celebration, displaying the Janus heads, playing Scottish folk music, possibly learning a Scottish dance, tasting some shortbread and reading a Scottish folk tale.

Welcoming the Chinese New Year

Objective
To celebrate the Chinese New Year by making appropriate animal masks.

Age range
Seven to eleven.

What you need
Assorted coloured papers and card, decorative materials, adhesive, scissors, paints and brushes.

What to do
Tell the children that the Chinese people have a traditional festival for celebrating new year – a 15 day period towards the end of January or beginning of February, according to lunar months. At this time families come together for special feasts and entertainment. Each year is associated with a particular animal (see below) and it is traditional for some people to make disguises in the form of these animals, as well as wearing Chinese dragon costumes.

Find out with the children the animal for the coming year and then guide them to make masks or simple costumes of this animal. Decorate the classroom (or school hall) with these items and/or make up a play or mime act featuring the animals. Hung-hay-fat-choy! (Happy New Year!)

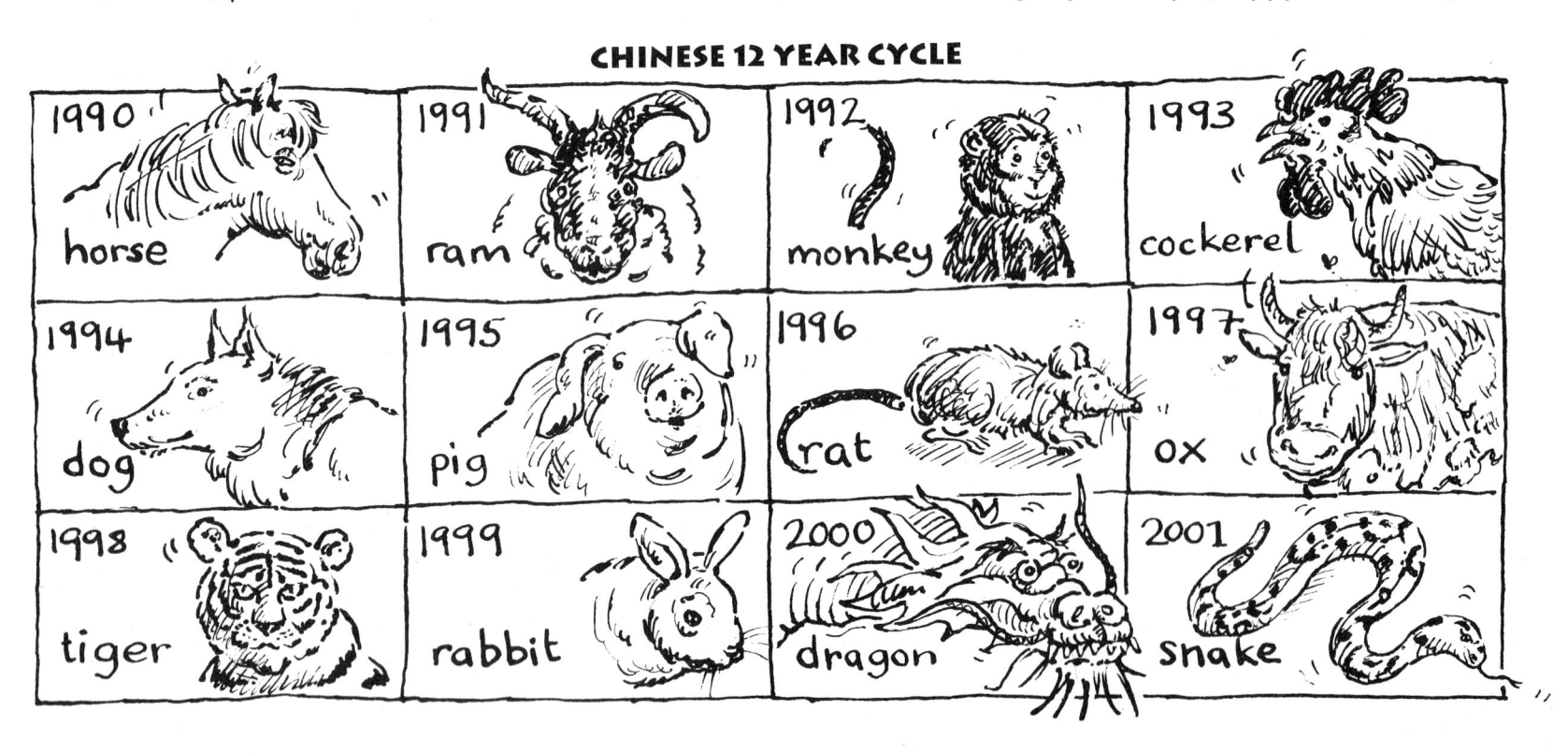

CHINESE 12 YEAR CYCLE

1990 horse	1991 ram	1992 monkey	1993 cockerel
1994 dog	1995 pig	1996 rat	1997 ox
1998 tiger	1999 rabbit	2000 dragon	2001 snake

New Year resolve

Objective
To think about and make formal New Year resolutions.

Age range
Seven to eleven.

What you need
Small pieces of writing paper, pens or pencils, scissors, drawing pins, a prominent display board.

What to do
Start off by discussing the general practice and purpose of making New Year resolutions. Ask the children to consider a resolution that might be relevant to what they do in the classroom. Advise them to think of some weakness or failing which they might make a new concerted effort to overcome. They should then write down these resolutions in a formal style:

At the beginning of this new year, _____,

I, _____

formally resolve that

I will _____
_____

These can then be pinned up in a prominent place and, from time to time, the children can assess how well they are fulfilling their resolutions.

New Year honours

Objective
To consider the practice of the New Year honours list and to make a class honours list.

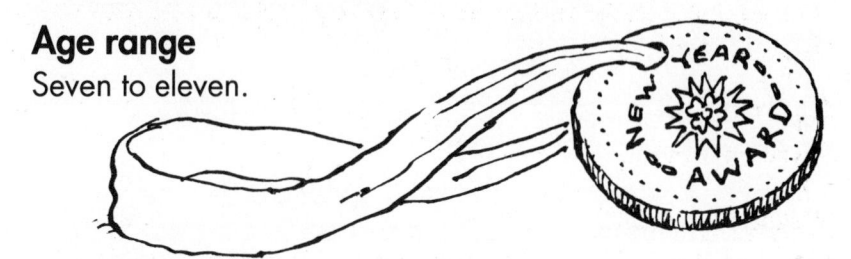

Age range
Seven to eleven.

What you need
Materials to make medals and trophies (card, foil paper and so on), paper, pencils.

What to do
First of all discuss what the children know about the New Year honours system and anyone who has just been honoured. Suggest that it would be a good idea if the class decided to make and present its own special awards. These could be both for public and local figures, particularly school staff and children. Discuss what these awards might be for and collectively make a list of them (maybe in smaller groups at first). Groups or individuals can then be assigned to making particular medals and trophies.

Copies of the list can then be given to each member of the class so that each child can put down the person of their choice for each category. The awards can be given and presented to the most popular name found in each category. This may be done in a special school assembly. If any outside public figures are given awards attempts should be made to send these to the recipients with a written explanation.

Years in orbit

Objective
To demonstrate how years succeed each other as the Earth completes new orbits.

Age range
Seven to eleven.

What you need
Information books about the solar system, a globe – preferably tilted on a stand, a flat large 'sun shape' to be dangled from a central point on the ceiling, coloured paper, thread, adhesive.

What to do
Ask the class the question, 'Can anybody explain what makes years go by?' Steer the discussion to focus particularly on the issue of the Earth making continual orbits around the Sun and how each orbit denotes the passing of another year. Demonstrate this by holding a globe and moving it in a circle around the dangling sun shape. Show, too, how the tilt of the Earth allows different amounts of sunshine to reach different parts of the world at successive stages of an orbit. The globe could be left dangling from the ceiling at some distance from the sun shape and then gradually through the year – say at the beginning of each month – it could be shifted so as gradually to make an orbit.

The children could make their own two-dimensional orbiting schemas, or year charts. For this they need to make large circular papers (after drawing round the classroom bin, perhaps) and colour a sun on the middle point. Then they will need to draw a much smaller ball shape to represent the Earth. This could be attached by a thin thread to the Sun and then made to orbit in circles. Older children could be challenged to work out how far the Earth moves each month – the same proportion as five minutes on a clock. The names of the months can then be marked in each five minute space.

Finally, pose the questions, 'Where does the orbit begin?' Of course, there is no natural beginning point and our New Year's Day is a completely arbitrary choice – different cultures therefore choose different times. The children could try to find out when different New Years take place.

Follow-up
Extend the idea to the orbits of other planets.

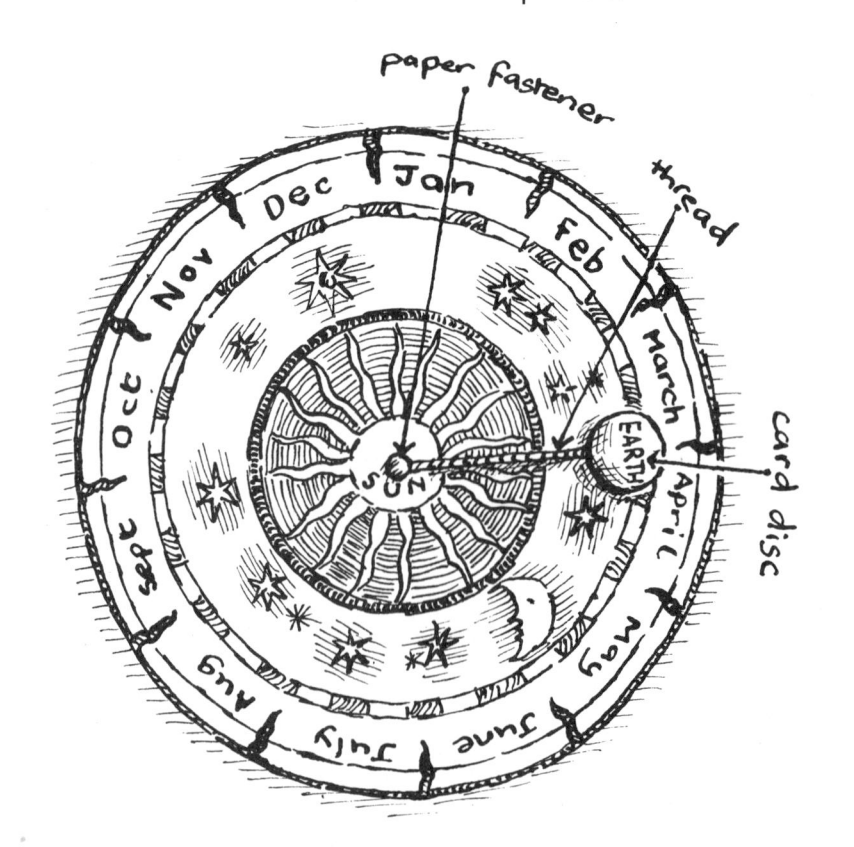

Winter nights

Objective
To think about different ways of spending long winter nights.

Age range
Seven to eleven.

What you need
Paper and pencils.

What to do
Ask the children first of all what they think are the main features that make winter different from summer. Focus the discussion particularly on aspects of winter darkness. With older children discuss the scientific explanation for this: the fact that the northern hemisphere tilts obliquely away from the Sun.

Then challenge the children to think of as many enjoyable ways of spending dark winter evenings as they can – even taking note of what other animals do. Ask them to list these different ways, maybe with a title with a set number – 12 (or 101!) enjoyable things to do on a winter's night.

Wake up! It's spring

Objective
To provoke ideas for creative writing and other new work.

Age range
Seven to eleven.

What you need
A few items typical of spring: some spring flowers, budding branches, eggshells and so on; pencils, writing paper.

What to do
Start off the lesson by proclaiming to the class the title of this activity, taking them by surprise, if possible, when they are in a relatively sluggish mood. Follow this by adding a few more emphatic statements along the lines of:
- Time to dust the cobwebs away!
- Time to make a change!
- Time to do better!
- Time for buds to burst!
- Time for birds to sing!
- Time for eggs to hatch! ....

and then see what other statements the children can add to this. If it is a typical spring day, you might add 'Time for us to be outside' and then take the children outdoors to a garden or park in order for them to see what else they can observe about the time of the year.

On returning to the classroom divide them into pairs, or small groups if they wish and ask them to jot down all the ideas they have for this theme – including a fuller interpretation like 'Time to feel ....', 'Time to wonder whether...', Time to look forward to ....' – particularly anticipating any future school event and anything new they would like to do. After a brainstorming session, ask the children to make their own individual poetic writings with the above title.

Follow-up
- Illustrate the writing to form part of a seasonal display.
- What small changes can be made in the organisation and routines of the class to sustain the idea of spring renewal? Organise a spring clean!

Spring sowing and growing

Objective
To demonstrate spring as a season of germinating seeds and new growth.

Age range
Five to seven.

What you need
Small flower pots – yoghurt pots with punctured bottoms, compost, a variety of seeds (dried beans, sunflower seeds, mustard seeds, orange pips or any seeds left over from already-opened seed packets), potted seedlings (tomatoes, cucumbers, bedding plants), thin sticks (split canes), rulers, pencils, peel-off labels, adhesive, watertight trays, a sunny window-sill.

What to do
Introduce this activity by asking the children about what happens in spring. Focus the discussion on the idea of spring being a special time for sowing and new growth. Tell the children that they are going to set up their own spring sowing and growing experiment, and ask them to bring in any seeds and seedlings: pips from fruit, dried beans or peas, bird seed, remains from old seed packets or any spare seedlings from gardens.

When the class has accumulated sufficient material, show them how the pots should be filled with compost and how smaller seeds are best sown near the surface whereas larger seeds should be buried slightly deeper in the soil. Each pot should be labelled and, preferably, stick a spare seed on this label (for later comparisons). Measuring sticks can be put in the pots and these should be marked at centimetre intervals from the soil level. When these procedures have been followed all the pots can be put on trays on sunny window-sills. Now all that needs to be done is very modest regular watering – possibly leaving some water in the trays over weekends – and the observation and recording of growth rates.

Follow-up
After four weeks or so, many of the seedlings will probably need transplanting. At this stage the classroom window-sill will become a less suitable place for growing some of the plants, so it may well be best to send these back to children's homes and gardens – unless there is a suitable school garden.

New days

The beginning of the school day is a prime learning time. The children should be at their freshest and most alert. They are also then likely to be more inclined and receptive to trying something new and different. Whatever has happened on the previous days they now have a chance to start again with a clean slate. Each new morning brings fresh opportunities.

It can also be a time of relative excitability while friends are greeted (especially after a weekend), but the children like to know what is expected of them and generally welcome having something to do straight away. For the teacher, on the other hand, this can be quite a frantic time with administrative details to attend to, individual problems to sort out and maybe a parent to speak to. So it is a good idea for the children to have preliminary activities with basic routines which they can undertake easily without needing much direction and assistance. Therefore, on the whole, the ideas suggested here are 'settling down' activities which do not require the children to wander about or go searching around.

Monday morning activities

Telling time

Objective
To develop oral confidence and competence, capitalising on a time when children often have much to say.

Age range
Five to nine.

What you need
A space for the class to sit together and talk.

What to do
Establish with the children that on Monday mornings the class has a regular 'Telling time' – a time when they listen while one child tells them about something interesting. They should soon get into the habit of being prepared for this occasion. The session could take a variety of forms, such as:
• *Show and tell* – an occasion for individual children to show, talk about and be questioned about something interesting or unusual that they have brought to school.
• *Say and tell* – an occasion for the children to say how they feel and why (Today I feel happy/sad/angry because ...).
• *Remember and tell* – an occasion for children to talk and be questioned about particular memories (times of surprise, loss, grief, anger, frustration, babyhood and so on).
• *Look forward and tell* – a session for anticipating future events, birthdays, outings ... and making plans.

Journals with a difference

Objective
To make written and illustrated entries into personal journals with a range of special focuses.

Age range
Seven to eleven.

What you need
Notebooks with lined and unlined pages, pencils.

What to do
Establish with the children that Monday morning is a time for making entries in a diary, journal or general book of personal writing and that this is an opportunity for them to write about ordinary and special things that may have happened to them just recently or over the weekend. Also tell them that, to help make their journals more interesting, each week you will be suggesting a particular theme or different way of making an entry. Each theme should be introduced with a short discussion to generate ideas. Make sure all the children have a clear idea what they may do and encourage them to write a title (a zippy one, if possible). Here are a few such suggestions:

Focus on the specific times and kinds of everyday occasion: waking up, Saturday shopping, Sunday lunch, going out, chores, best/worst TV programme, bedtime.

Focus on persons and relationships: me and my mother or father/brother/sister/cousin/grandparents/friends/pets.

Focus on feelings: 'Today I'm feeling ... because ...', 'When I feel sad/happy/lonely/excited/hungry...'

Use a particular opening line: 'Did you see ...?', 'Guess what! ...', 'You'll never believe it but ...'

Make fictional/spoof entries: stories full of imaginary events.

List: a number of things which you didn't do and one thing you did do.

Discuss and comment upon events or issues in the news: internationally, nationally or locally.

Make entries in the form of drawings: accompanied by captions or speech balloons.

Make general musings: 'Dear Journal, I'm sorry I can't think of anything to say', 'If only ...'

Make some entries deliberately brief and succinct: choosing just three adjectives to describe a weekend.

Chart the week

Objective
To make charts planning classroom management and principal curriculum schedules for the forthcoming week.

Age group
Seven to eleven.

What you need
A large piece of paper marked with a grid, smaller (A4) grid papers, a chalkboard, pencils.

What to do
In the first part of this activity the children will make a chart which sets out special classroom responsibility holders for the week (librarian, plant tenders, animal keepers, weather recorders, personal assistants to the teacher for errands and so on, and outlines the day to day main curriculum schedule along with any other special events such as birthdays and visits. This can then be put on the main classroom notice-board.

In the second part, children can make their own small schedules, putting in special personal reminders (such as if they need to bring anything extra to school on particular days) and noting if they have any extra responsibilities.

Monday news-sheet

Objective
To compile topical general news-sheets.

Age range
Seven to eleven.

What you need
A3 or A2 white paper, lined paper cut to a planned column width, adhesive, scissors, pencils.

What to do
This is an activity which is best used as a regular exercise at the beginning of each week, alternate week or month. A regular system should therefore be established for producing the news-sheet.

Divide the paper into a number of subject sections and appoint different pairs of children to edit and compile these sections on each occasion. These sections might include 'main news', 'sports', 'food', 'out and about' (accounts of family trips and so on), 'entertainment and TV', 'interviews', 'gossip', 'jokes and cartoons', 'letters' and 'official' (notices from staff). Begin production with a general discussion about the main items of topical news, and then ask every child to contribute an article or picture for one of the sections. The section editors could also commission particular contributions.

Follow-up
- Reproduce (with photocopy reduction) copies of the news-sheet for distribution (and sale?) through the school.
- The news-sheets could be filed chronologically to provide a record of the school year.

Monday moods

Objective
To reflect on the idea of a 'Monday morning feeling' and use this to develop creative writing.

Age range
Nine to eleven.

What you need
A chalkboard, pencils, writing paper.

What to do
Raise the idea of a 'Monday morning feeling' with the children and talk about different ways they or other people may feel it. List some of the suggested ideas and evocative vocabulary on the board. Then ask the children to see if they can write the words of a song beginning 'I've got that Monday morning feeling …' or other words along those lines.

Follow-up
Ask the children to compose music for their lyrics.

Language activities

Listings

Objective
To make lists of different kinds of words and phrases.

Age range
Five to eleven.

What you need
A chalkboard, dictionaries, fiction and non-fiction books, notebooks, pencils.

What to do
Tell the children to list as many words as they can which belong to a specified 'category'. The number of possible word categories is immense, so requests can be made appropriate to a wide range of ages and abilities. Suggestions for such listings are offered here in three broad groupings.

Spelling groups
– Words beginning with a particular letter or two letters.
– Words containing particular vowels or vowel combinations.
– Words with particular double vowels or consonants.
– Words with particular letter groupings: *ough, ion, ght, chr, sch, str, thr, ure, que, ing, ble, cle*.
– Words with silent letters: *tongue, friend, know, gnat*.

Parts of speech
– Nouns (common and proper) naming different phenomena: places, people, animals, trees, foods, clothes, objects.
– Adjectives to describe particular nouns: apples, cats, cars, moods, size, colour, texture, school, the weather.
– Pronouns referring to different persons and nouns.
– Verbs indicating actions and states of being (what people/cats/cars/clouds/things do).
– Adverbs qualifying actions, descriptions (ways of working, sitting, thinking).
– Prepositions indicating directions and positions (ways of hiding something).

Vocabulary groups
– Words that rhyme: with, for example, *friend, said, all, bite, caught*.
– Homophones: words with identical sounds but different spellings *(son/?, to/?, for/?, size/?, ate/?)*.
– Homonyms: words with same sound or spelling with different meanings: *(peer/peer, lean/lean)*.
– Synonyms: words with the same meaning.
– Words with common roots: *school, scholar, scholastic*.
– Words associated with a particular subject – jargon.

* For a full list of such groups see *Good Words* by William Edmonds (Kingfisher Books, 1993).

Letter of the day

Objective
To draw special attention to particular letters of the alphabet, their formation and their occurrence in words.

Age range
Five to nine.

What you need
Paper or notebooks and pencils.

What to do
Establish with the children that from time to time you will be choosing a special 'letter of the day' and that for this they will need to do a particular activity at the beginning of each day. The activity will obviously vary according to the age and abilities of the children and might include any of the following exercises:
• finding and maybe noting down words beginning with that letter;
• practising the correct formation of this letter, printed or cursively;
• finding and noting down as many words as possible which begin with this letter but each having a different second letter:
• finding and noting down a succession of words where this letter occurs in successive positions;
• making jokey alliterative phrases or sentences, perhaps tongue-twisters.

Bright and early

Objective
To savour the sensation of being outside first thing in the morning and to represent this in writing and drawings.

Age range
Five to eleven.

What you need
Somewhere to take a short walk outside school, a chalkboard, paper, pencils.

What to do
Tell the children that you are all going to take a short walk together to look and listen to what's going on outside at the beginning of the day. Before going out, ask them to be particularly observant of the different things people are doing, the animals they see, the traffic that is about, the things they see growing, the effects the weather may be having, the main background sounds, and anything else which they think might be special this morning.

When the children come back to the classroom have a brainstorming session recalling significant observations and note salient descriptive vocabulary on the chalkboard. Then ask the children to make their own lists of comments (possibly combining with partners) about the experience of being out bright and early, and to shape these into poetic pieces of writing. Younger children could just collect and note a few descriptive words, or make single caption sentences to accompany an illustration.

Spelling teases

Objective
To detect and correct spelling errors and confusions.

Age range
Seven to eleven.

What you need
A chalkboard, notebooks, dictionaries, pencils.

What to do
Put a list of commonly misspelt words, or a text including misspellings, on the board and ask the children to try to rewrite the words correctly, using dictionaries, if necessary. It is a good idea if each set of words contains a similar type of error, for example: changed first or last letter, changed vowels, two letters switched, missing letters, superfluous letters, single letters when they should be doubled or vice versa, examples of particular kinds of mistakes currently found in the class.

Follow-up
- Ask the children to complete texts where words have had one or two letters substituted with asterisks.
- Ask the children to decipher or make anagrams.
- Ask the children to decipher or make coded messages where a particular system of jumbled letters has been applied, or where a number of homophones have been used.

thier   there
scool   school

Substitution word play

Objective
To write a series of repeating sentences or phrases where each time a word or two is changed, added or deleted.

Age range
Seven to eleven.

What you need
A chalkboard, paper or notebooks, pencils.

What to do
Write a simple sentence or phrase on the chalkboard. For example:

It is a beautiful day today

Discuss with the children how this sentence might be altered by changing any of the words, adding new words or deleting one or two of them. Write on the chalkboard two or three sentences where such changes have been made. For example:

It is a ghastly day today.
Henry is a ghastly boy today.
Henry was a ghost today.
Henry was a ghost buster.

When the children have all understood the process, wipe off all the examples except the first line and ask the children to write their own sequences of sentences with word substitutions.

Test reading

Objective
To read first chapters of books to find out and note who, and what, they are about.

Age range
Seven to eleven.

What you need
A collection of fiction books that have chapters, notebooks, pencils.

What to do
Put a book or two on each desk and ask the children to read the first chapter of one book to find and note who are the main characters in the book and what they mainly do.

Follow-up
- Tell the children to skim through the rest of the book and to summarise the plot.
- Tell the children to write their own second chapters to follow the first chapter.

Writing in style

Objective
To practise writing repeated lines of text and letter patterns focusing on particular handwriting qualities.

Age range
Seven to eleven.

What you need
A chalkboard, plain paper, lined backing paper, pencils or pens.

What to do
Ask the children to make repeated copies or variations on a model line of writing you have written on the chalkboard. Emphasise that this is an exercise to concentrate on perfecting their handwriting. Here are a few ideas on which the model lines can be based.

Just look at this beautiful handwriting!

making letters all of a regular size

lots of lovely letter l l l l l l l l l l

ooooooooooh aaaaaaaaaah

seeeeeeeeee sawwwwwwwwww

perfect peas put in proper places

words spaced nice and evenly apart

writing as fast as I possibly can

CAPITAL LETTERS IN STRAIGHT ROMAN STYLE

Word of the day

Objective
To draw special attention to particular new words, dwelling on their meanings, uses and spellings.

Age range
Seven to eleven.

What you need
A chalkboard, dictionaries, paper, pencils.

What to do
Choose a word for the day and write it in clear big letters on the chalkboard at the beginning of the day. The word could be chosen for several different reasons and could well be relevant to a lesson later on. For example, the word could be:

- a moral/educational concept such as *loyalty, patience, perseverance, forgiveness, generosity, gratitude* or *consideration.*
- a scientific concept like *buoyancy, reflection, magnetism, astronomy, geology* or *germination.*
- a linguistic term like *adjective, conjunction, onomatopoeia, punctuation, sentence, paragraph, homophone* or *poetry.*
- a more general term like *magnificent, abundance, fascination, population, voyage* or *expectation.*

Tell the children to copy out this word clearly for themselves and then to find, think about and note down dictionary definitions of it. Ask them to write a sentence using the word explicitly in context and to practise spelling the word by 'look and cover' techniques.

Follow-up
- Refer to the new word as much possible through the day and snap test the children on its meaning and spelling.
- Ask the children to use any of the letters of the word of the day to make up as many other words as they can.
- After some discussion, or other work about the meaning of the word, ask the children to write an acrostic poem, writing a sequence of sentences each beginning with the successive letters of the word.

Alphabet ordering

Objective
To practise putting words into alphabetical order.

Age range
Seven to eleven.

What you need
A chalkboard, notebooks and pencils.

What to do
Write a sentence on the board and ask the children to put all its words into alphabetical order, such as:

Please can you put all the fifteen words in this sentence into exact alphabetical order?

Follow-up
• Challenge the children to write a single sentence in words beginning with as many different letters of the alphabet as possible.
• Ask the children to make an alphabetical index to go with a completed notebook.

Dictionary search

Objective
To give practice in searching for words and meanings in dictionaries.

Age range
Seven to eleven.

What you need
A chalkboard, dictionaries, notebooks, pencils.

What to do
Provide the children with a list of words for which they have to find dictionary definitions. Such a list could be related to a certain topic which is being, or is about to be, studied in the classroom. It could include words which are commonly confused, such as homophones. Or it could involve searching for multiple definitions of a particular word.

"It was a hot day and Arthur was asleep on his doorstep."

Story starts

Objective
To look at and also create different ways of starting stories.

Age range
Seven to eleven.

What you need
A selection of story-books, notebooks or paper, pencils.

What to do
Ask the children to look at the opening sentence in a number of story-books and to select and note down the three sentences that they like best. Ask them to read some of their choices to the class and discuss with them the various merits of these choices.

This could be followed up, maybe at a later time, by asking the children to compose and write a few different first lines for stories on a range of subjects (dragons, aliens, tearaways, forests, tunnels, holiday adventures and so on).

Follow-up
Ask the children to write full stories following on from openings suggested above or from openings suggested by you (bizarre exclamations or leading questions, for example).

Read, quote, illustrate

Objective
To read part of a book, quote a typical short passage and draw an illustration to go with it.

Age range
Seven to eleven.

What you need
A selection of fiction books, paper or notebooks, pencils.

What to do
Ask the children to read a chapter of their current book, or to read for a set period of time, and afterwards to select a representative sentence or two from the story to quote in writing. They should then draw a suitable illustration to go with this and also note the title and author of the book.

Follow-up
• Make a display or class book of the illustrated quotations.
• Make a quiz involving the identification of such quotations.

Mathematical activities

Grouping

Objective
To count quantities of small objects in different number groups.

Age range
Five to eleven.

What you need
Trays (box lids) with assorted different numbers (from 20 upwards) of small identical objects (counters, small cubes, plastic coins, nails), paper, pencils.

What to do
Divide the class into pairs and put a numbered tray on each table for each pair of children. Tell them to arrange the objects in groups of two and to note how many whole groups are made, and then to do the same with groups of three, four and so on. Provide the children with, or show them how to make, charts to record their findings, like the one shown below.

Tray ( )	
Group size	lots
2	
3	
4	
5	

Follow-up
Use the same material for directly dividing the quantities into different numbers of equal heaps.

Shape seeking

Objective
To look for and create examples of principal regular two-dimensional shapes within the classroom.

Age range
Five to seven.

What you need
Templates of squares, rectangles, triangles and circles; paper, pencils.

What to do
Divide the class into four groups and give each group a number of templates of one of the four shapes: squares, rectangles, triangles and circles. Tell the class that you want the members of each group to find, collect together if possible, and record as many different examples of their shape as they can find in the classroom. Tell them that they can also look for pictures of such shapes in books and make arrangements of items (like pencils, rulers, scissors, pieces of string) into these shapes (this will assist the seekers of triangles and squares especially). Display the findings.

Follow-up
Use similar procedures to identify three-dimensional shapes.

Number of the day

Objective
To focus on one number, finding different ways of making it or breaking it down.

Age range
Seven to eleven.

What you need
A chalkboard, counting apparatus (optional), notebooks, pencils.

What to do
Select a particular number (one which has several factors, one related to the day's date, a fraction or a number chosen at random) and ask the children to work out and note down as many ways they can of splitting it into different quantities, using counters or other counting blocks if they wish. Show the children how to present their numerical groupings as equations, or as sums which all have the same answer, using addition and multiplication procedures.

Follow-up
Tell the children to represent a particular number in different ways as variously-shaped blocks of squares.

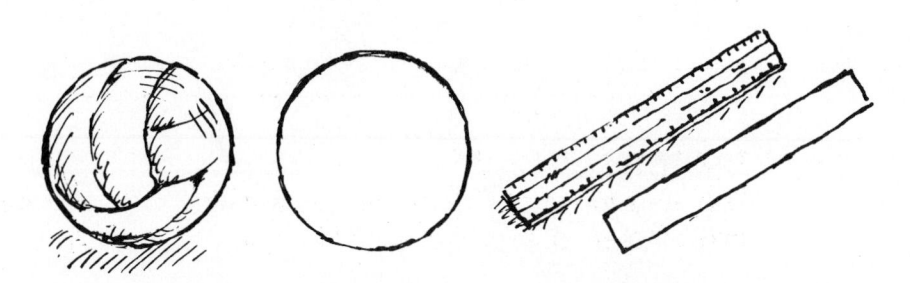

Equal areas

Objective
To demonstrate on grids how the same area can be shaped in a variety of ways.

Age range
Seven to eleven.

What you need
Grid paper marked off in centimetre squares, pencils.

What to do
Give the children pieces of grid paper and ask them to make as many different shapes as they can with the same area – 18 square centimetres, for example. Encourage older children to use diagonal lines which will involve counting half squares as well.

Lots and lots

Objective
To practise looking at, working out and learning multiples of any small number.

Age range
Seven to eleven.

What you need
Copies of the 'Lots and lots' worksheet (photocopiable page 107) with a chosen number inserted in the title box, pencils.

What to do
Provide each of the children with a copy of the worksheet. Make sure they understand the instructions and then ask them to fill in the sheet, starting off by colouring the relevant border numbers.

Grid patterns

Objective
To create patterns/pictures on grids as specified by co-ordinate references.

Age range
Seven to nine.

What you need
A chalkboard, squared grid paper, pencils, coloured pencils.

What to do
On the chalkboard write the co-ordinate references for a simple pattern or basic picture on a grid, perhaps directing that different squares be shaded in particular colours. Give each of the children a piece of grid paper and ask them to number off the squares vertically and horizontally starting from the bottom left-hand corner. Then tell them to shade in the squares according to the references given on the board to discover what image they create.

Follow-up
Suggest to the children that they make their own design on grid paper and then write down the co-ordinate references for it (which they could pass on for someone else to try out).

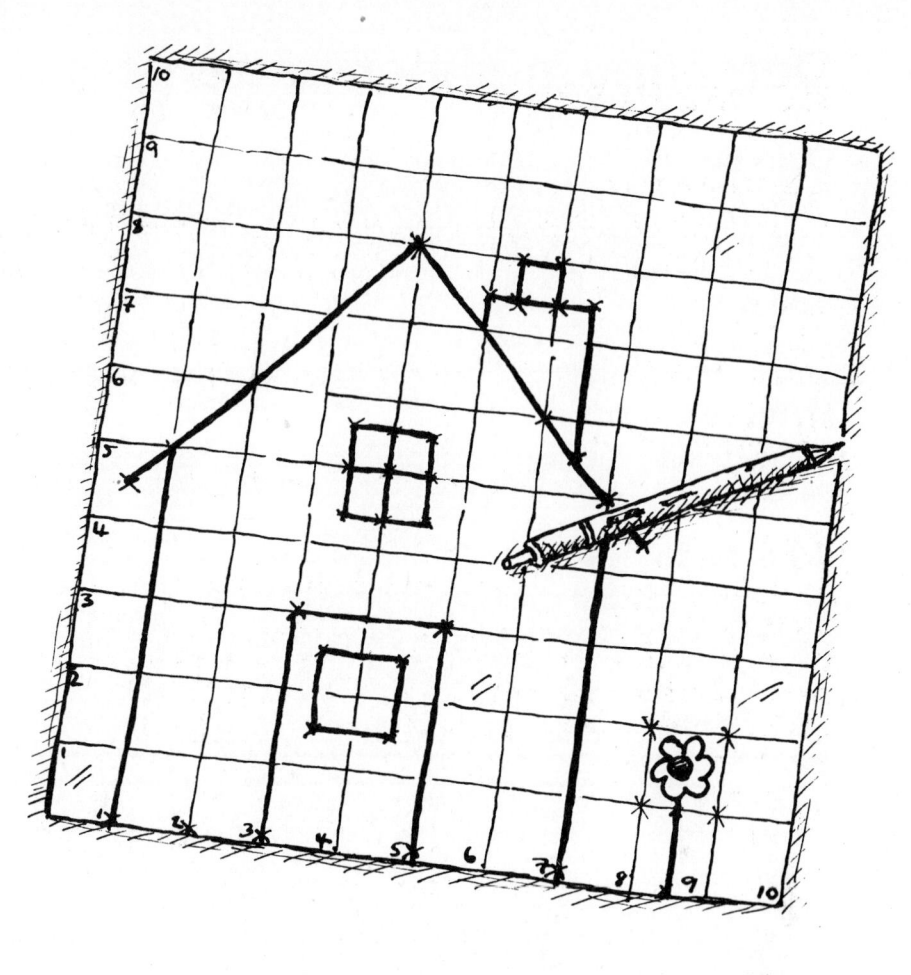

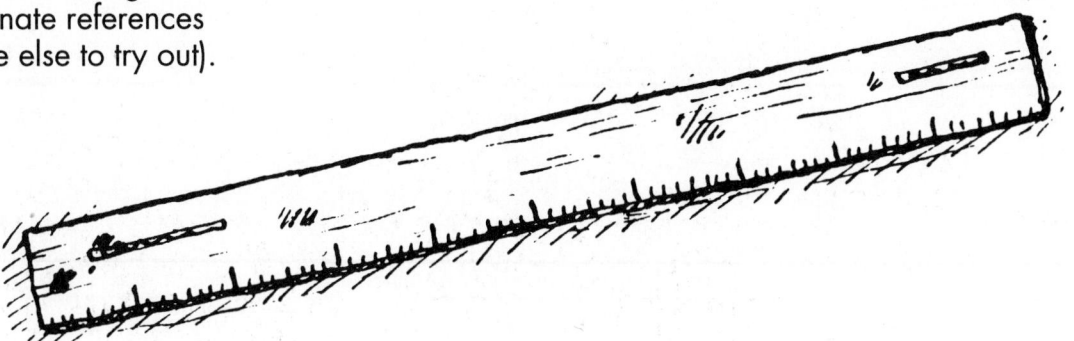

Detecting number patterns

Objective
To carry out a series of numerical calculations and find patterns in the sequence of answers.

Age range
Seven to eleven.

What you need
A chalkboard, counting apparatus (optional), notebooks, pencils.

What to do
Write on the board a numbered list of numerical calculations, appropriate to the development level of the class, whose solutions follow a particular numerical sequence or progression (numbers of a multiplication table, numbers increasing/decreasing by certain regular or regularly-changing intervals). Ask the children to do these calculations and to see if they can identify and explain the pattern that the answers follow. Detecting the pattern should provide them with a means of assessing how accurate they have been.

Once they have completed the listed calculations the children could go on to make further calculations which continue the pattern of answers.

Follow-up
Instruct the children to continue a particular numerical sequence as far as they can in a short specified time. (Count on as far as you can in 3s, 15s, 99s, ¾s, for example.)

Morning surveys

Objective
To collect data and to make quantitative surveys of observable or recordable phenomena (a traffic or TV viewing survey, for example).

Age range
Seven to eleven.

What you need
Pencils, plain paper, clipboards, squared paper for making block graphs.

What to do
Tell the children that they are going to carry out a survey which involves collecting quantifiable information available that morning and then presenting it in a clear form such as a block graph. This could be a survey of different kinds of traffic passing the school gates during a particular time, of different means of transport used by the children that morning, of different cereals eaten at breakfast or foods brought to school, of TV programmes watched last night or any number of popularity surveys.

Design and carry out the survey, assigning different groups of children to count different aspects if necessary, then collate and record the results.

Follow-up
- Make a follow-up comparative survey at a different time of day or time of year or with different sample material. Do the results differ? If so, can the children give any reasons for why this may be?
- Ask the children to think of alternative ways of recording their results and data.

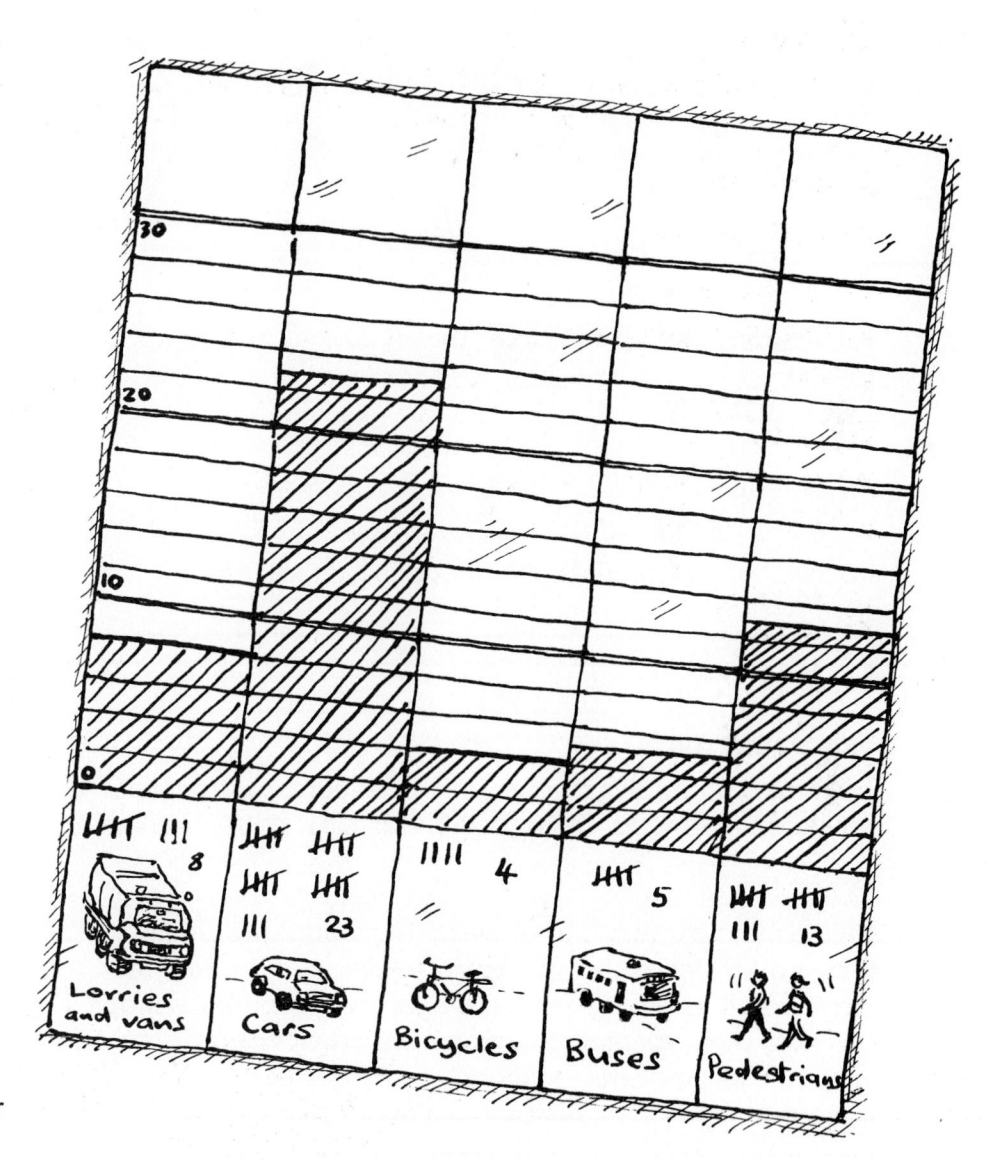

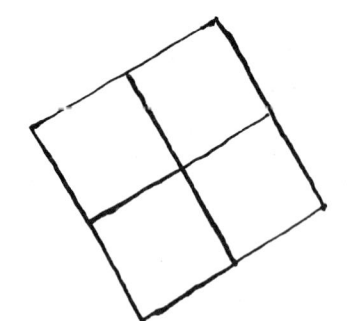

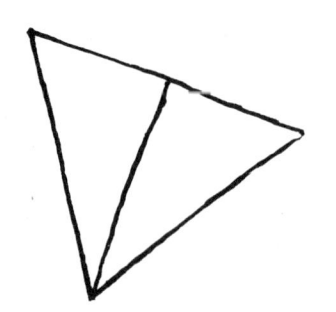

Shape shading – fractions

Objective
To divide regular shapes into particular fractions and distinguish the divisions by shading.

Age range
Seven to eleven.

What you need
Templates of regular shapes such as squares, rectangles, equilateral triangles, hexagons and circles; paper, pencils.

What to do
Divide the class into four or five groups and give each group a few templates of one of the different shapes. Tell the children to use the template to draw two or three shape outlines. Then ask them to find different ways of dividing the shapes into particular fractions (say ¼ and ¾), to label these and make them distinct with contrasting shading. Encourage the children to find as many different ways as they can of demonstrating the same proportional divisions with each shape.

Long lines

Objective
To draw and measure long ruled lines on small pieces of paper.

Age range
Seven to eleven.

What you need
Postcard-sized pieces of paper, rulers, pencils.

What to do
Tell the children to see if they can draw a continuous ruled line which makes turns and is of a specified total length (say 1m/100 centimetres) on their postcard-sized piece of paper. Show them how each section should be drawn and marked to an exact number of centimetres. Ask them to consider and experiment with different ways of making the line fit into the small space – zigzags, loops or spirals, for example.

When the children have achieved this first objective successfully, ask them to draw and measure the longest ruled line that they can in the same space, or perhaps in a differently-shaped small space.

Coded messages

Objective
To decode and encode simple messages.

Age range
Seven to eleven.

What you need
A chalkboard, paper, pencils.

What to do
Write a coded message on the board such as:

3 15 14 7 18 1 20 21 12 1 20 9 15 14 19!

14 15 23   13 1 11 5   25 15 21 18

15 23 14   13 5 19 19 1 7 5

Ask the children to see if they can decode this message. They should work out fairly quickly that the numbers represent the letters of the alphabet in their order and that they have been requested to make their own message.

Follow-up
• Make messages using sums whose solutions are the number/letter correspondences above.
• Make messages with codes in which letters have been switched with others a set number of places along in the alphabet order.
• Make messages where letters have been randomly switched. Solving such a code will entail consideration and possibly investigational analysis of letter frequencies in any normal text.

Problem challenges

Objective
To solve challenging problems requiring logical thinking and numerical operations.

Age range
Seven to eleven.

What you need
A chalkboard, paper and pencils.

What to do
Present the children with a challenging mathematical problem to solve, writing the principal details out for them on the board to focus the attention of the whole class. For example:
- If six (or any number) people meet and shake hands, how many handshakes are there?
- Find change for £1 using 12 (or any number) coins.
- In Farmer Giles' farm there were some hens and some pigs. Farmer Giles counted all their legs. There were 34. What was the highest number of pigs he might have had? What was the highest possible number of hens?
- A frog fell down a well 10 metres deep. She climbed up one metre each hour, then fell back half a metre. How long did she take to get out?
- 1 2 3 4 5 6 7 8 9 = 100. Insert addition and subtraction signs to make this a true statement. You can combine adjacent figures to make two-digit numbers if you think it necessary.

New starts through the day

The first part of this chapter consists of 'Special Assignments' – tasks specifically designed for individuals or small groups:
• To make use of spare times (when other work has been finished early).
• To provide curriculum support to individuals with particular needs.
• To make effective use of resources in limited supply (like computers, calculators, weighing scales).
• To develop independent working skills, maybe by having a 'special assignments' time for the whole class doing a range of different activities.

The activities in this section centre on 18 major learning processes: making, sorting, drawing, inventing, spelling, researching, picturing, puzzling, weighing, imagining, observing, scientific testing, using a calculator, measuring, questioning, word processing, listening and reporting. They are essentially self-sufficient tasks based on simple worksheets (see photocopiable pages 108 - 125) requiring no more than standard classroom resources. A short list of 'further assignment' ideas is presented at the end of each activity.

It is suggested that a classroom bank of special assignment sheets be made by adapting and/or copying the photocopiable samples, and also by making use of the further assignment ideas. The principles behind each assignment generally apply to the whole primary age range but adjustment of the tasks to fit particular levels will be needed. For the youngest children spoken directions will often be more suitable.

Most of the individual activities should take between 10 and 30 minutes to carry out. But, of course, as starting points they could well lead to more extended work. At the end of this section are some extra ideas for two-minute and ten-minute tasks.

Special assignments

Make a magic castle

Objective
To construct a model to particular specifications.

Age range
Five to nine.

What you need
Special Assignment sheet 1 on photocopiable page 108, assorted junk construction materials or construction kits.

What to do
Follow the instructions on Special Assignment sheet 1. This involves making a magic castle with four thick walls, gaps for a door and spy-holes, four corner towers and a mast with a flag. The result can then be displayed, maybe alongside others that have been completed so that different construction techniques can be compared.

Further assignments
- *Make other models*
Invite the child to make models of other objects such as boats, dens, monsters, machines, robots and so on.
- *Make instructions*
Invite the child to make instructions/plans to build such models.
- *Perform engineering feats*
Invite the child to achieve particular constructional objectives: very tall stable towers, strong bridges to span specified gaps, tripod constructions and so on.
- *Build houses*
Invite the child to construct houses from different materials – straw, sticks, paper, card, bricks, particular construction kits – and to compare their qualities.
- *Make boxes*
Invite the child to design and make boxes from nets.

Sort six counters

Objective
To sort objects into groups and/or patterns.

Age range
Five to nine.

What you need
Special Assignment sheet 2 (photocopiable page 109), an assortment of counters, a pencil.

What to do
Follow the instructions on Special Assignment sheet 2. This involves sorting out and recording as many different patterned arrangements of six counters as possible.

Further assignments
- *Sort 24 counters (or 12, 30, 36, 48 and so on)*
Invite the child to sort 24 counters into two, three, four, six, eight and twelve groups and to record the groupings (with dots, rings or numbers).
- *Sort odds and ends*
Invite the child to find and record ways of sorting out a tray of odds and ends (buttons, paper-clips, pins and so on) into two groups, three groups, four groups.
- *Sort logic shapes*
Invite the child to find and record different ways of sorting out a kit of logic shapes into different groups.
- *Sort into order*
Invite the child to sort out a particular part of the classroom, such as tidying a bookshelf and seeing that the books are arranged in alphabetical order by author's name.
- *Sort by computer*
Invite the child to use a data processing system to collate and sort out basic personal information such as ages, heights, weights, interests and preferences of class members.

Draw and count

Objective
To do drawings as illustrations to words, numbers and so on.

Age range
Five to seven.

What you need
Special Assignment sheet 3 (photocopiable page 110), pencils, coloured crayons or felt-tipped pens.

What to do
Follow the instructions on Special Assignment sheet 3. This involves drawing particular numbers of windows, doors, birds, roses and chimneys on an outline house and then counting up the total number of details.

Further assignments
• *Draw numbers*
Invite the child to draw and count one funny face, two funny cats, three funny pigs, four funny sausages and so on.
• *Initial letter drawings*
Invite the child to draw something or a number of things that begin with a particular letter.
• *Read and draw*
Invite the child to illustrate a short sentence. For example:
The pink cat sat fast asleep on the green mat.
• *Draw and caption*
Invite the child to draw and name three examples of: different shapes, pets, fast foods, fast cars, dinosaurs and so on.
• *Illustrate a story*
Invite the child to choose a favourite story and to do an extra illustration for it.

Invent a new toy or game

Objective
To make and understand the nature of an invention.

Age range
Five to eleven.

What you need
Special Assignment sheet 4 (photocopiable page 111), a tray and/or box of materials such as thread, pins, paper-clips, lolly sticks, cotton reels, card, corks; sticky tape, adhesive, felt-tipped pens and basic craft tools.

What to do
Follow the instructions on Special Assignment sheet 4. This involves creating a new toy or game with some corks, paper-clips, thread, pins and card.

Further assignments
- *Design an invention*
Invite the child to design an invention: a new harmless animal trap; a dog or cat house; a new way of coming to school; a chair, bed or school desk with extra gadgets.
- *Invent new uses*
Invent and list alternative uses for ordinary objects - ten different ways of using a book, pencil or paper-clip.
- *Recycle*
Invite the child to invent ten ways of re-using a jamjar, plastic bottle, tin can, newspaper or toilet roll.
- *Invent the future*
Invite the child to design blueprints for future methods of travel, future dwellings, foods or entertainment.

Spell the magic

Objective
To practise spelling words.

Age range
Seven to eleven.

What you need
Special Assignment sheet 5 (photocopiable page 112), pencils.

What to do
Follow the instructions on Special Assignment sheet 5. This involves spelling as many different words as possible on a square grid framed by the word *abracadabra*.

NB *Abracadabra* itself can be made to appear 12 times on this square, but this severely limits the range of other words that might be inserted. So it is advised that children experiment with this themselves.

Further assignments
- *Cast your own spells*
Invite the child to take a tray of letters (such as Scrabble pieces or letters printed on small squares) and to make up as many words as possible, maybe in a crossword pattern.
- *Spell magic rhymes*
Invite the child to compile a list of words that rhyme with one particular chosen word such as *spell* itself, or *rhyme, word, friend, witch, potion, eye, trick*.
- *Alternative spellings*
Tell the child that an American President, Andrew Jackson, once said that 'It is a damned poor mind that can only think of one way to spell a word.' Then ask the child to find as many different ways as possible of spelling a particular word such as *word* itself, or *ceiling, crazy, magic*.
- *Spell and cluster*
Invite the child to make a list of words which all include a particular cluster of letters like *ough, ion, sch, gh, ght, ea, th, ph, ing, ie, ies, ei, nt, str, our*.
- *Spell it out*
Invite the child to spell out his or her name (or any other more complicated word) by writing a word for each letter of the name: *A for ape, n for naughty, n for never*.

Researching parrots

Objective
To find out particular information by researching in books.

Age range
Seven to eleven.

What you need
Special Assignment sheet 6 (photocopiable page 113), a library, pencils.

What to do
Follow the instructions on Special Assignment sheet 6. This involves gathering information on parrots: a picture to copy and details about varieties, diet and other facts of interest.

Further assignments
- *Research pictures*
Invite the child to find (and perhaps copy) a picture of a tiger, pterodactyl, tractor, tomahawk, turnip....
- *Research names*
Invite the child to find ten names of wild flowers, African animals, famous women, wind instruments....
- *Research facts*
Invite the child to find out three (or any number of) curious facts about windmills, Timbuktu, hedgehogs....
- *Research origins*
Invite the child to find out about the origin of cheese, chalk, paper, fireworks, television, crisps....
- *Research people*
Invite the child to find out what people, such as Julius Caesar, Galileo, Marie Curie, Grace Darling or Yuri Gagarin were famous for.

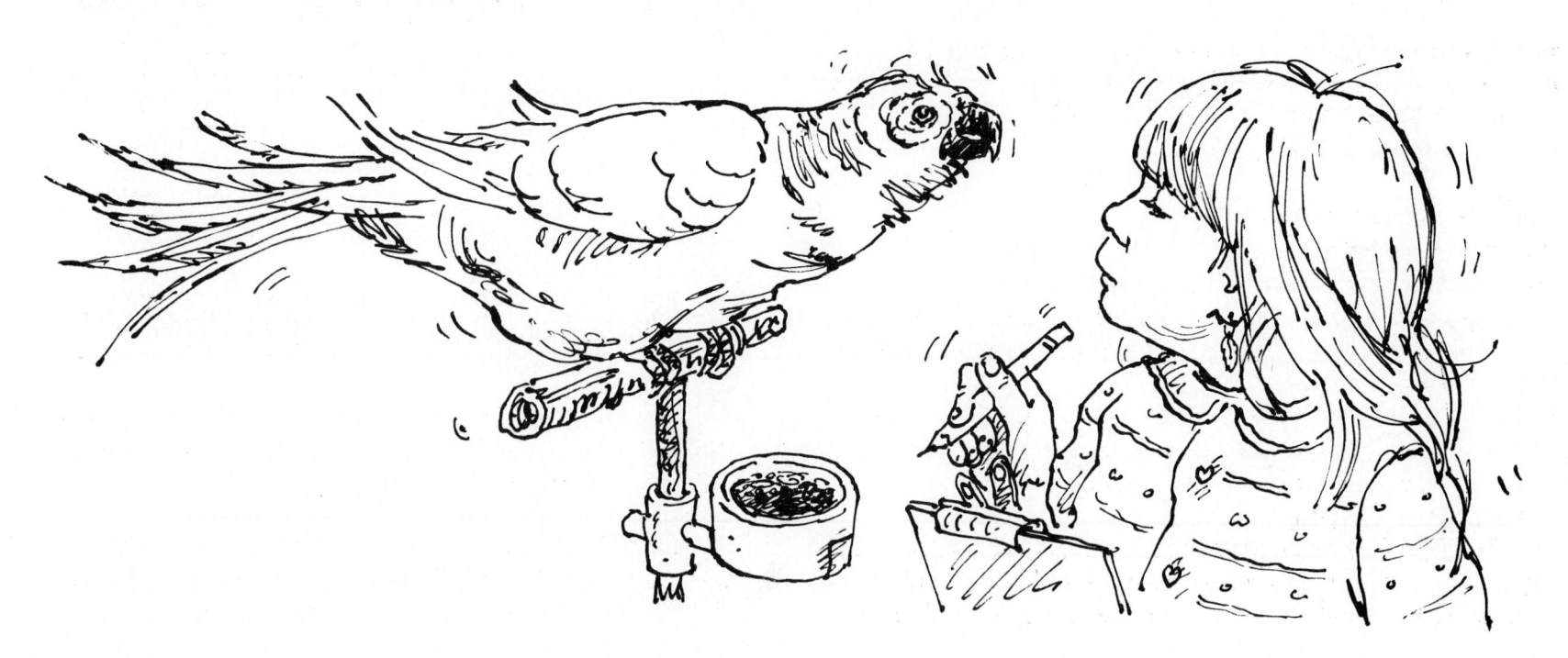

Picture to shape

Objective
To promote challenging and original picture making.

Age range
Five to nine.

What you need
A copy of Special Assignment sheet 7 (photocopiable page 114), a selection of pieces of paper cut into slightly unusual shapes, paints, paint brushes, crayons.

What to do
Follow the instructions on Special Assignment sheet 7. This involves colouring pictures or patterns in a variety of shapes and then painting a larger scale picture on an unusually-shaped piece of paper.

Further assignments
● *Picture the scene*
Invite the child to picture literally the scene in another place – at their grandparents', a holiday place, the meeting of a cat and mouse or any other rivals, for example.
● *Imagine and picture*
Invite the child to think of a particular abstract concept such as happiness, fear, excitement, boredom and then to represent this sensation in the form of a picture or pattern of colours.
● *Picture with one shape*
Invite the child to take a template of a particular simple shape like a circle, square or triangle, and then to draw round it several times – adapting each outline to create a different image. For example: the same triangle could become a hat, a sail, a roof, a mountain or a face.

Puzzle with cubes

Objective
To solve and create a range of puzzles.

Age range
Five to eleven.

What you need
A copy of Special Assignment sheet 8 (photocopiable page 115), a set of construction cubes, pencils.

What to do
Follow the instructions on Special Assignment sheet 8. This involves working out and checking how many cubes there are in the construction illustrated on the card. A pyramid puzzle can also be built and investigated.

Further assignments
• *Puzzle and spell*
Invite the child to solve and make some anagram puzzles or spelling alternatives – *puzzell, puzal, puzzle*.
• *Puzzle with words*
Invite the child to do or make crossword and wordsearch puzzles.
• *Code puzzles*
Invite the child to decode coded messages, such as when letters are substituted for those of the alphabet in reverse order.
• *Number puzzles*
Invite the child to complete magic number squares. For example:

3	10	2
	5	
		7

• *Dotty puzzles*
Invite the child to draw as many squares as they can on a 4 x 5 grid of dots without taking the pencil off the paper, and without retracing or crossing any drawn line.

Weigh a box of goods

Objective
To investigate the comparative weights of assorted objects in the classroom.

Age range
Seven to eleven.

What you need
Special Assignment sheet 9 (photocopiable page 116), balancing weighing scales, quantities of particular materials like cotton reels, conkers, marbles, building bricks, small books, pencils.

What to do
Follow the instructions on Special Assignment sheet 9. This involves putting a small box of a particular kind of goods – chalks, crayons, counters or coins – on one side of a pair of scales and then finding different ways of balancing this with particular quantities of other objects.

Further assignments
• *Set weights*
Invite the child to find and record several different assortments of things that weigh a particular set weight: a kilo, 500 grams and so on.
• *Weigh the contents of a desk*
Invite the child to arrange and record the contents of their desk in order of weight with the help of scales.
• *Weigh and balance coins*
Invite the child to find different ways of balancing various quantities of coins of different denominations.
• *Weigh tubs of this and that*
Invite the child to fill a number of identical plastic tubs (old ice-cream or margarine tubs) to exactly the same level with different materials and then to find out, record and order their weights.
• *Weigh yourself*
Invite the child to weigh him/herself and to find out (by weighing and calculating) what quantity of a particular classroom object (a dictionary, say) would make the same weight.

Imagine you're a mouse

Objective
To stimulate a 'flight of imagination'.

Age range
Five to nine.

What you need
Special Assignment sheet 10 (photocopiable page 117), pencils.

What to do
Follow the instructions on Special Assignment sheet 10. This involves imagining what it is like to be a mouse and writing about where you live, what you eat and what adventures you have had.

Further assignments
- *Imagine being someone important*
Invite the child to imagine and describe being a teacher, prime minister, somebody old, famous or rich.
- *Imagine and draw*
Invite the child to draw an imaginary creature, place or other world.
- *Imagine a perfect world*
Invite the child to imagine an ideal world. Ask them to write a succession of lines that each begin 'Imagine …'

> Imagine a perfect world
> Imagine if no one was poor and hungry
> Imagine …
> Imagine …

83

Observe and draw

Objective
To make a skilful observation.

Age range
Five to eleven.

What you need
Special Assignment sheet 11 (photocopiable page 118), drawing paper, pencils, and possibly some colouring materials.

What to do
Follow the instructions on Special Assignment sheet 11. This involves looking closely at somebody else working and making an observational drawing.

Further assignments
- *Observe and remember*
Invite the child to look at a collection of objects on a table or a shelf and then to turn round and try to recall everything that was there or be questioned about it.
- *Observe differences*
Invite the child to observe and list the differences between two members of class or two fairly similar objects.
- *Observe and record*
Invite the child to observe and record particular things from a classroom window – anything moving, signs of life, colours or shapes, for example.
- *Observe and imagine*
Invite the child to look at a good picture – a reproduction of a classic painting, for example – and to imagine being in it. Then ask them to describe the experience either orally or in a piece of creative writing.

Test with a magnet

Objective
To carry out a scientific test.

Age range
Five to nine.

What you need
Special Assignment sheet 12 (photocopiable page 119), a magnet, a pencil.

What to do
Follow the instructions on Special Assignment sheet 12. This involves using a magnet to test a range of objects or materials in the classroom for magnetic attraction. If objects are magnetic how strong is the attraction?

Further assignments
- *Test for water porosity*
Invite the child to put drops of water on a variety of objects and to observe whether the water soaks in or runs off.
- *Test for buoyancy*
Invite the child to test and record how well a variety of objects float.
- *Test for temperature*
Invite the child to use a thermometer to record temperatures in order to find the warmest and coldest parts of the classroom and playground.
- *Test for insulation*
Invite the child to put a variety of materials near a radiator to find which insulate against the heat.
- *Test for strength*
Invite the child to test materials (a variety of bags, for example) to see how easily they tear, their capacity to support increasing weights and to withstand knocks.
- *Test for light*
Invite the child to devise a way for testing relative light and darkness in different parts of the classroom and school.

Calculate number rows

Objective
To use a pocket calculator effectively.

Age range
Seven to eleven.

What you need
Special Assignment sheet 13 (on photocopiable page 120), a pocket calculator, a pencil.

What to do
Follow the instructions on Special Assignment sheet 13. This involves using the calculator to add together the sequences of numbers from 1 to 10, 11 to 20, 21 to 30 to see if a pattern emerges, which enables the successive sequences to be predicted quickly without using the calculator.

Further assignments
- *Big calculations*
Invite the child to find and record different ways of reaching the biggest number possible on the calculator.
For example: 9 + 90 + 900 + 9000 and so on
or: 11111111 x 9 =
- *Calculate a number story*
Invite the child to make and record the minimum number of steps they can find between any two numbers using all four basic operations.
For example: 1 to 100 ([1] [+10] [x20] [÷2] [-10] [=])
- *Calculate number chains*
Give the child a collection of numbers (5 49 100 17 ...) and ask them to find an operation that will link the chain (+44 +51 −83).
- *Calculate doubling up*
Invite the child to choose a number and use the calculator to see and record how far he or she can go on doubling it.
For example: 2x2=( ) x2=( ) x2=( ) x2=( ) ...

Measure the distance

Objective
To measure a particular distance.

Age range
Five to nine.

What you need
Special Assignment sheet 14 (photocopiable page 121), string, rulers, a tape measure, a stopwatch or any other measuring devices, pencils.

What to do
Follow the instructions on Special Assignment sheet 14. This involves thinking about and noting down two different methods of measuring the distance from the classroom to the school office. The children then select a suitable method, make an initial estimate of the distance, do the actual measuring, check it and finally record it.

Further assignments
- *Measure and compare alternative routes*
Invite the child to measure and compare alternative routes around the school which have the same starting and finishing point.
- *Estimate local travelling times*
Invite the child to estimate and list travelling times for a variety of local distances and methods of travel.
- *Take measurements of desk contents*
Invite the child to measure the dimensions of items in desks – in terms of millimetres or ant-paces.
- *Measure with maps*
Invite the child to measure distances between particular places on maps using rulers and marking off scale lines.

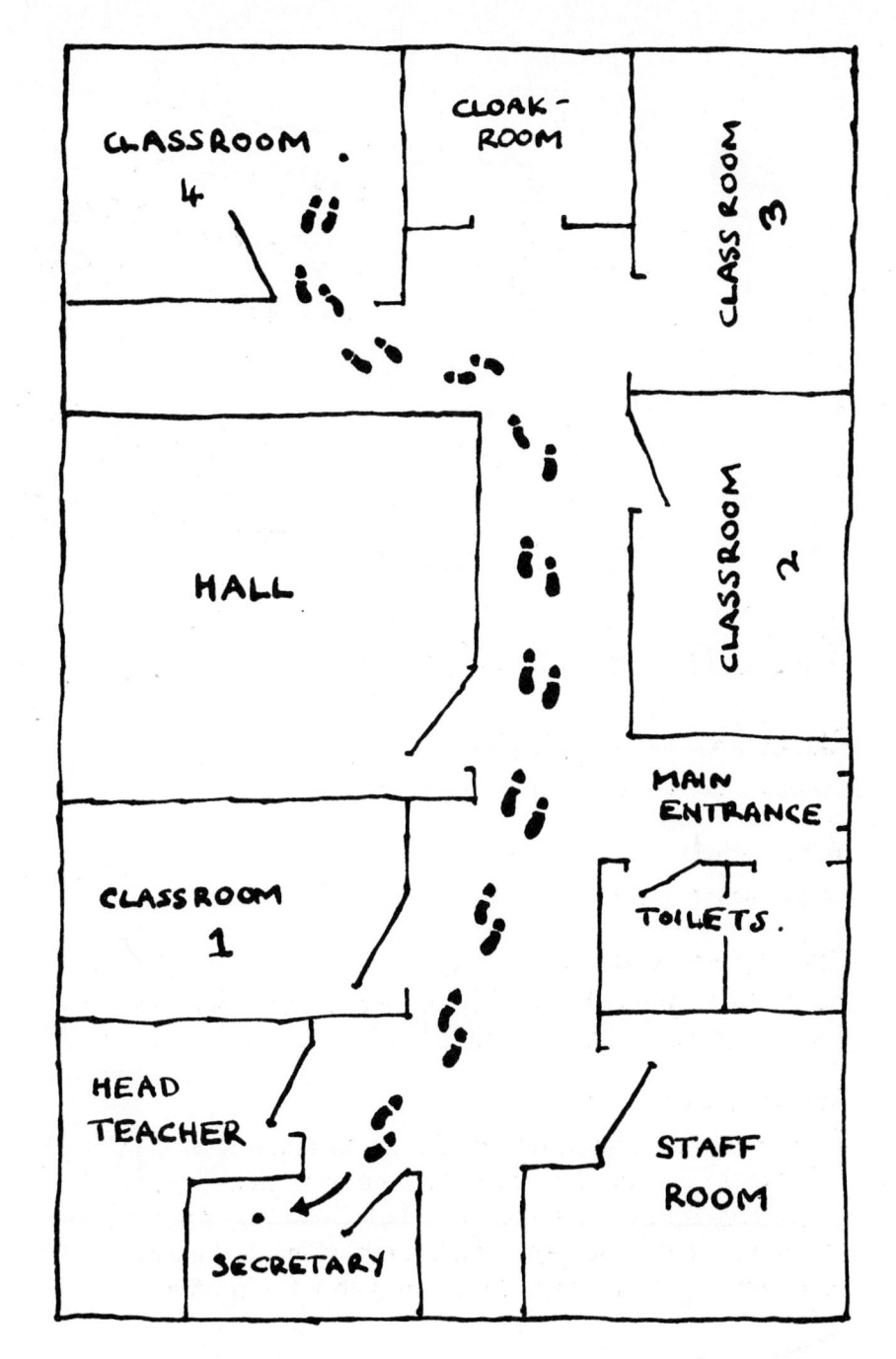

LONDON
What is the capital of Great Britain?

LONDON

In which city would you find the Houses of Parliament and Tower Bridge?

Question and quiz

Objective
To promote quizzical thinking and questioning.

Age range
Seven to eleven.

What you need
Special Assignment sheet 15 (photocopiable page 122), pencils.

What to do
Follow the instructions on Special Assignment sheet 15. This involves thinking of and writing down five questions which all have the same answer, such as the name of a place or person, animal or anything you can think of. Such questions might be rhetorical or they might make up a genuine puzzle.

Further assignments
• *Questions about numbers*
Invite the child to make a wide range of numerical questions (sums) that all have the same number answer.
• *Questions for interview*
Invite the child to prepare a short list of questions with which to interview another person in the school.
• *Class quiz*
Invite the child to write a number of quiz questions on a particular subject to be used for a class quiz.
• *Suggestion questions*
Invite the child to write 'How about …?' or 'Why don't …?' questions for a classroom suggestion box.

Of which city was Dick Whittington Lord Mayor?

LONDON

What did the Romans call Londinium?

LONDON

Which city was nearly destroyed by the Great Fire in 1666?

LONDON

Process a story

Objective
To make effective use of a computer word processing system.

Age range
Nine to eleven.

What you need
Special Assignment sheet 16 (photocopiable page 123), access to a computer word processing system.

What to do
Follow the instructions on Special Assignment sheet 16. This involves typing a short circular story and then using the 'copy and paste' procedures to extend it several times.

Further assignments
• *Process a class saga or soap opera*
Invite the child to find the disk on which their story has already been started and to insert a further instalment – at the end, the beginning or anywhere in the middle of the story.
• *Process an expanding story*
Invite the child to type a simple sentence, such as 'The chicken crossed the road' and then to insert words to add details about the chicken, the crossing and the road. Then ask them to add sentences at the beginning and the end to set the scene and describe the consequences.
• *Process and disguise*
Invite the child to change adjectives and adverbs in a descriptive story which has already been put on to the disk. Keep successive printouts of the story as a record of the changing versions.

Listen in

Objective
To encourage attentive listening.

Age range
Seven to eleven.

What you need
A copy of Special Assignment sheet 17 (photocopiable page 124), a pencil.

What to do
Follow the instructions on Special Assignment sheet 17. This involves listening for a while to the background conversation and noises going on in a classroom and writing down a sample selection of remarks and words overheard – in the form of a poem, maybe.

Further assignments
- *Listen outside*
Invite the child to listen and list sounds heard outside.
- *Listen for pleasure*
Invite the child to choose a story or music tape and listen to it just for pleasure.
- *Music to my ears*
Invite the child to think of and list some of the things he or she likes to hear – these can include both words and music.
- *Listen to me!*
Invite the child to write down or tape record the experience of being 'buttonholed'.

Report on the weather

Objective
To investigate a particular situation and make a report.

Age range
Seven to eleven.

What you need
A copy of Special Assignment sheet 18 (photocopiable page 125), thermometer, compass, pencil.

What to do
Follow the instructions on Special Assignment sheet 18. This involves making and recording observations about cloud cover, the position of the sun, temperature, signs of rain, wind conditions and visibility. It will help with this activity if the class has already had some collective experience of monitoring weather conditions, so that the procedures are relatively routine.

Successive reports should be displayed or kept together to maintain a continuous record of weather conditions.

Further assignments

- *Nature report*

Invite the child to make a detailed report on the current state of any classroom animals or plants – recording details of size, growth, colour, shape, state of health.

- *Classroom report*

Invite the child to make a report on the current state of the classroom: principal activities being carried out, noise level, tidiness, temperature, ventilation and so on.

- *Playground report*

Invite the child to make a report on the current conditions in the playground: its particular areas, weather conditions, the amount of litter present, current popular playtime games and activities.

- *News report*

Invite the child to make a true or fictional report for a class news-sheet or radio broadcast about a recent event.

- *Progress report*

Invite the child to assess his or her current individual performance in main subject areas.

Two minute tasks

Objective
To carry out a task that takes just two minutes.

Age range
Five to eleven.

What you need
Two Minute Task tickets (photocopiable page 126), a two minute timer or a stopwatch – a classroom clock with a second hand will usually do.

What to do
Use photocopiable page 126 to make 12 tickets, each containing one task. Carry out one of these tasks. These are a range of tasks which involve counting in different numbers, word reading counts, physical tests, observations, chores and so on. Some of these are timed tests and some of them are just brief activities that do not have to be timed exactly.

Ten minute tasks

Objective
To carry out a task that takes just ten minutes.

Age range
Five to eleven.

What you need
Ten Minute Task tickets (photocopiable page 127), a visible clock or watch, a pencil.

What to do
Use photocopiable page 127 to make 12 tickets, each containing one task. Carry out one of the ten minute tasks. The tickets involve a variety of tasks such as reading, making lists, counting, checking spellings, learning poems, sketching, doing good deeds and playing word games.

Coming together again

To conclude, here are just a few starting points to encourage all the children to start afresh with a new and generally short activity. Most teachers and classes will have their own special routines for making use of spare times together – a class novel to continue, a song or two to sing, special reading times, question times, joke times, show and tell times or variations of party games like 'hangman' and 'Simon says'. The following ideas provide some extra opportunities to engage the active attention of the whole class and to assert a renewed sense of shared purpose.

Secret numbers

Objective
To play a game, involving numerical thinking, to find out a secret number.

Age range
Five to eleven.

What you need
No specific requirements.

What to do
Ask one child to think of a number between 1 and 100 (older children could be asked to think of a number between 1 and 1000 or more). Tell the rest of the class that they have to try to find out what this number is by asking up to ten questions which can only have a 'yes' or 'no' answer. If someone finds the number in less than ten questions, then that person can take a turn at thinking of a number. If not, the 'thinker' may reveal his or her number and be questioned again on another number.

Follow-up
• Challenge the children to find a fool-proof 'system' to find out the secret number with a minimum number of questions.
• Ask all of the children to think of a secret number and tell them to follow a sequence of numerical operations, starting by adding a few specific numbers to their secret numbers and then subtracting the secret number from the total. Carry on a few more operations and then see how many children finish with the correct common final number. (For example: add 1, add 2, add 3, add 4, subtract your first number, multiply by 10, subtract 99: the final number has to be 1).

Secret operations

Objective
To play a game that requires the participants to find out a secret numerical operation.

Age range
Seven to eleven.

What you need
A chalkboard, chalk.

What to do
The best way to introduce this game is for the teacher to decide on a secret operation (say x 2, + 3) and then to ask the children, in turn, to suggest any number to test. The suggested numbers are written on one side of the board and opposite each of these the teacher writes the number resulting from his or her secret operation. For example:

$$5 \longrightarrow 13$$

$$99 \longrightarrow 201$$

$$10 \longrightarrow 23$$

and so on

After five sets of numbers have been given, ask the children to see if they can puzzle out the secret operation. If they cannot do it readily you should continue to provide more examples of the operation at work until the secret is discovered. Once the children have understood the procedures of this game they can be asked individually to provide the secret operations themselves.

Secret words

Objective
To play a game to find out secret words by unravelling their spellings.

Age range
Seven to nine.

What you need
A chalkboard, chalk.

What to do
Ask the children each to think of a secret word, to write it down somewhere and, if necessary, to check its spelling. Then ask one of the children to start calling out letters of the alphabet in any order. As soon as the caller names the first letter of one or more of the secret words, the holder or holders of these words have to identify themselves. The caller carries on naming letters in order to try to identify a second, a third letter and so on until he or she has unravelled the whole of one secret word. The idea is to carry on briskly until as many secret words have been revealed as possible in the time available. To help the children become familiar with the procedures it may help if the teacher acts as the caller on the first few occasions. If the first caller is a child, he or she can rejoin the class to see if his or her secret word is discovered.

Hot seat

Objective
To let members of the class publicly question a child volunteer about a particular sphere of knowledge (set multiplication tables or spellings, for example).

Age range
Seven to eleven.

What you need
A raised chair.

What to do
This activity is appropriate if children are in the process of memorising a particular piece of knowledge, such as a multiplication table or a set of spellings. The children's confidence is built up because for most of the time they are the question masters.

One of the children volunteers to take the 'hot seat' and the teacher invites the rest of the class to ask ten questions. Any child asking a question must know the answer to the question he or she is asking. If the volunteer in the 'hot seat' succeeds in answering all ten questions correctly then he or she can be presented with a special class award.

Solve the problem

Objective
To pose and solve a logical problem collectively.

Age range
Seven to eleven.

What you need
Scrap paper and pencils.

What to do
Present to the children the 'canoe problem':

Two men and two boys want to cross a river.

Their canoe will take one man or two boys.

How do they all get across?

Give the children approximately five minutes to consider and try to find solutions to this problem working individually, with partners or in small groups. Then pool their findings and see if together you can establish the necessary nine separate crossings (*1* Two boys across. *2* One boy back. *3* One man across. *4* One boy back. *5* Two boys across. *6* One boy back. *7* One man across. *8* One boy back. *9* Two boys across).

Follow-up
Present the rather similar problem of a farmer taking a fox, a rabbit and a cabbage across a river carrying no more than one at a time and never leaving the fox alone with the rabbit or the rabbit alone with the cabbage.

97

Co-ordinating

Objective
To play a game that helps to develop a good understanding of co-ordinates.

Age range
Seven to eleven.

What you need
A chalkboard, chalk.

What to do
Draw a grid of about 12 by 12 squares on the board. Then number the squares on the left-hand side and across the top. Divide the class into two groups and explain that they are going to play a game similar to noughts and crosses where teams compete to be first to cover five squares in a row – horizontally, vertically or diagonally. Members of each team then take turns to fill a square with the team's symbol by calling out the two co-ordinate numbers (first the vertical and second the horizontal number). The teams carry on filling the square alternately until one team succeeds in filling five squares in a row in any direction.

Telling stories

Objective
To invent and recount a story that continues from one teller to another.

Age range
Five to nine.

What you need
No specific requirements.

What to do
The teacher should start by announcing the opening of the story, such as 'Once upon a time there was …' and ask various children to name an assortment of characters for the story. Then, maybe with some prompting, allow a succession of children to build up a story or sequence of anecdotes about these characters. Each member of the class could be asked to say what happens on the following day in the story, to introduce a new place that the story reaches or to introduce a new character to be met and dealt with.

Follow-up
Record these stories with a tape recorder and add accompanying sound effects.

Brainstorms

Objective
To collect and generate ideas about a particular subject as a prelude to a more thorough study or a stimulus for creative work.

Age range
Five to eleven.

What you need
A chalkboard or big sheets of paper, chalks or large felt-tipped pens.

What to do
Tell the class that they are going to see how a large number of people thinking together can come up with a lot of ideas, and that they are going to do this by extending the principle that two heads are better than one, to include everybody in the room. Firstly, announce the subject matter or general question, for example 'Dragons' or 'What's the great fascination of dragons', and then ask the children to say the first thoughts or answers that come into their head. The children should understand that their first thoughts need only be tentative and that no comments or explanations are necessary. The key words of the suggested themes should be written in a random list on the board or on big pieces of paper by the teacher or by children who have volunteered to act as scribes. These could also be presented as a spider diagram as shown below. The brainstorming of ideas should continue until it begins to exhaust itself.

Follow-up
- Make simple posters or big notices of 'brainstorms' on particular subjects.
- Underline and number the principal ideas that emerge from the brainstorming session. These could then be represented in a more ordered way and used as headings for a more developed investigation.

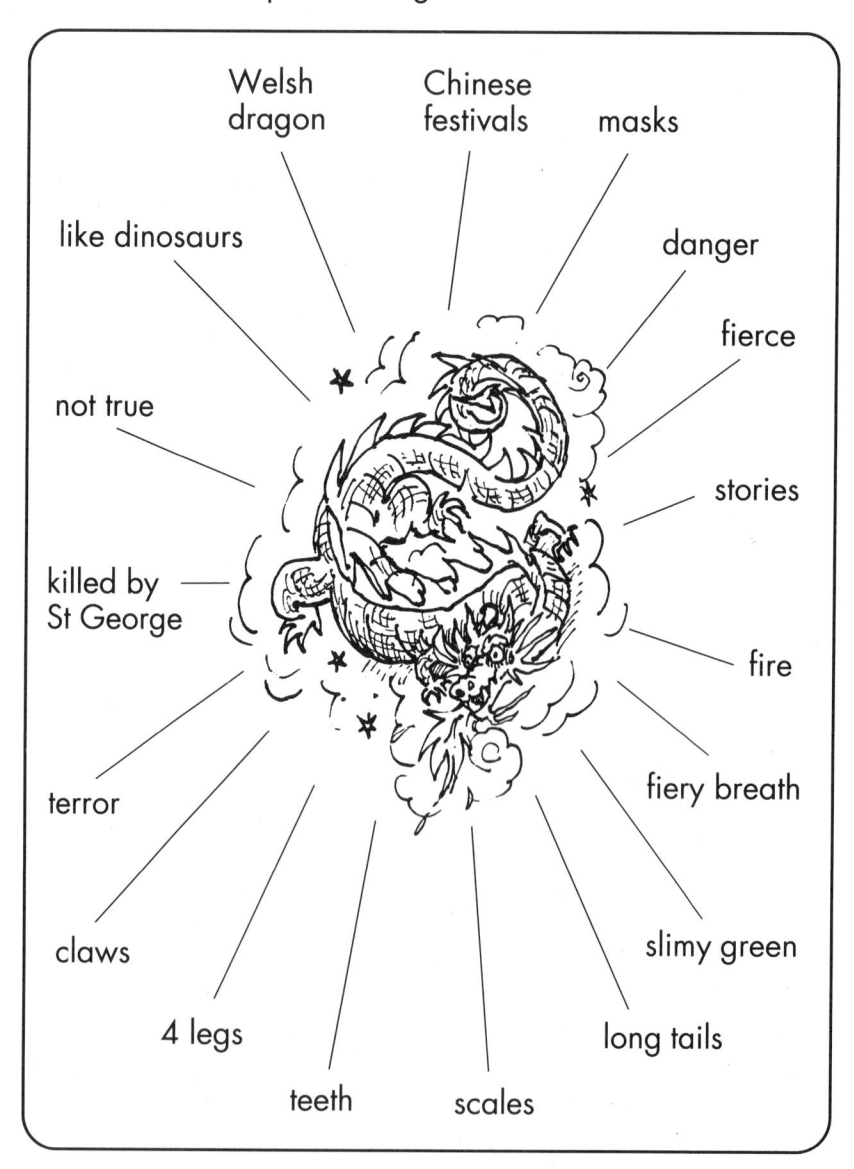

Golden silence

Objective
To introduce a period of restful and productive silence, maybe as an antidote to a previous more noisy or lively session.

Age range
Five to eleven.

What you need
Pencils, paper and crayons.

What to do
Here is a small selection of different ideas for achieving and reflecting on this objective.

- *Silent colouring*
Give the children some drawing paper and ask them to draw, in silence, a picture or pattern using only golden colours – yellow and orange. This could be an image centred around the word SILENCE.
- *Silent communication*
Tell the children that they are going to spend a period of time acting as if they were deaf and dumb, and that during this time they can only communicate by writing.
- *Sounds unheard*
Ask the class to be totally silent and to write down all the things they can't hear and form these into a poem.
- *Listening to a pin drop*
Ask the children to put their heads on their desks and shut their eyes while one child goes around the room occasionally dropping a pin on a variety of surfaces. The child has to see how many times the pin can be dropped without the whole class signalling that they have heard.
- *Distant noises*
Ask the children to be silent for a short period of time and to list all the noises they hear outside the class.
- *Silent timing*
Ask the children to try to wait for exactly one minute after a starting signal and then to raise their hands when they think the time is up. Repeat this two or three times to see if the children's timing becomes more accurate.

Reproducible material

Who are we?, see page 9

Who am I?

My name is _____

I live at _____

What do I look like? _____

_____

_____

_____

Where do I belong? (names of family, school, class, clubs)

_____

_____

I am crazy about _____

_____

I get bored when _____

_____

My pet hates are _____

_____

The funniest thing that ever happened to me was

_____

_____

_____

I like dreaming about _____

_____

Last year I _____

_____

Today I _____

_____

When I leave school _____

_____

This page may be copied for use in the classroom and should not be declared in any return in respect of any photocopying licence.

Facts and figures, see page 13

Questionnaire

Name _____

Age _____ years _____ months

How many brothers? _____

How many sisters? _____

How many grandparents? _____

Measurements

Height: _____

Weight: _____

Foot length: _____

Arms stretched: _____

Skills

Games that you know how to play:

_____

_____

_____

Musical instruments played or being learned:

_____

_____

Languages spoken: _____

_____

Special tricks: _____

_____

_____

Cooking skills: _____

_____

_____

This page may be copied for use in the classroom and should not be declared in any return in respect of any photocopying licence.

Facts and figures, see page 13

Experience

Places or countries visited: _____

_____

_____

Famous people seen: _____

_____

_____

Shows attended: _____

_____

_____

Unusual creatures seen: _____

_____

_____

Favourites

Food: _____

_____

Football team: _____

_____

TV programme: _____

_____

Book: _____

_____

Computer game: _____

_____

Outdoor game: _____

_____

Pop star: _____

_____

This page may be copied for use in the classroom and should not be declared in any return in respect of any photocopying licence.

Signs of Autumn, see page 39

Date and time	Temperature recording	General weather conditions	Colour of leaves on particular tree	Fruits observed	Observations of animal behaviour (pets, birds, insects, caterpillars)	Other signs

This page may be copied for use in the classroom and should not be declared in any return in respect of any photocopying licence.

Lots and lots, see page 64

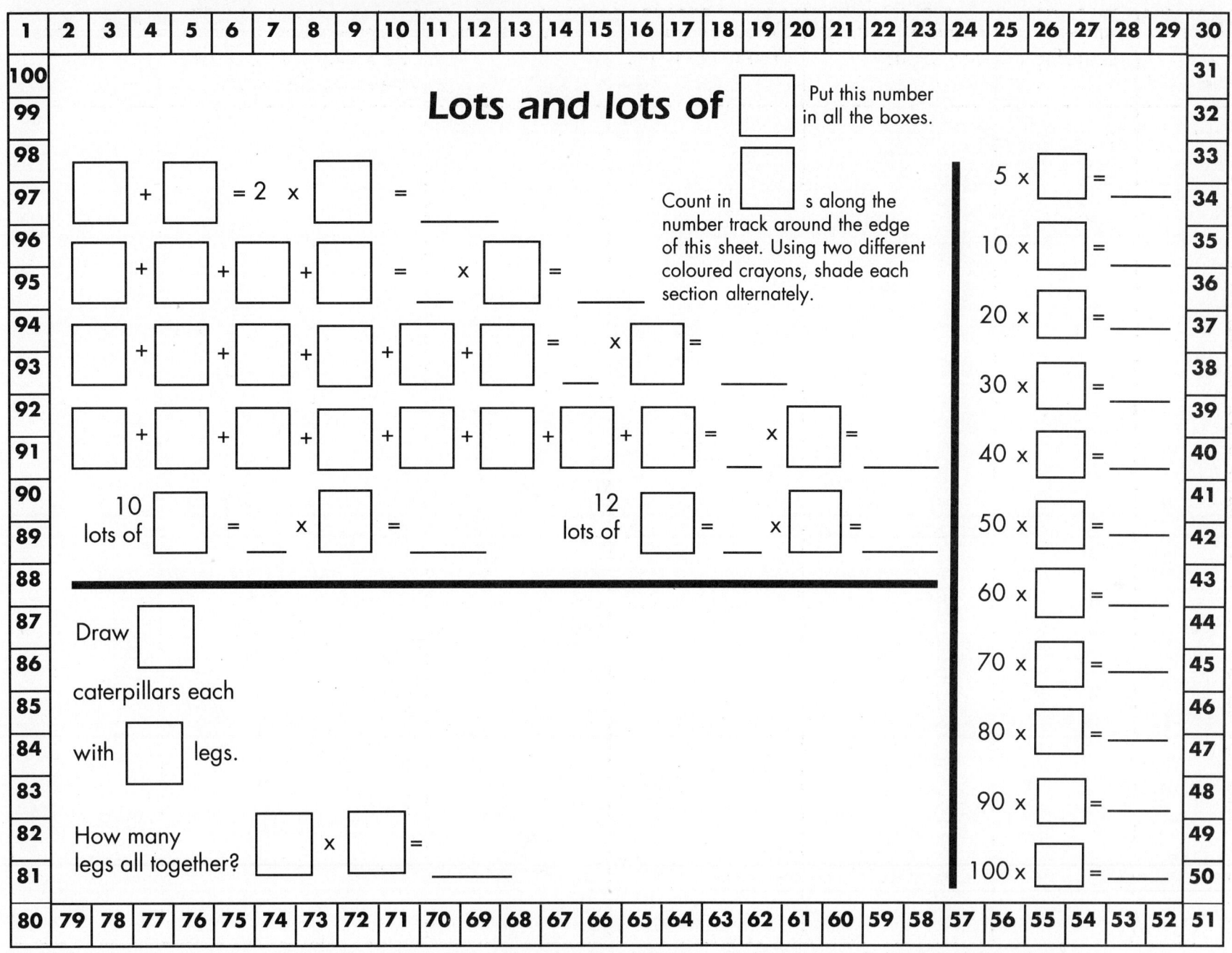

| 1 | 2 | 3 | 4 | 5 | 6 | 7 | 8 | 9 | 10 | 11 | 12 | 13 | 14 | 15 | 16 | 17 | 18 | 19 | 20 | 21 | 22 | 23 | 24 | 25 | 26 | 27 | 28 | 29 | 30 |

Lots and lots of ☐

Put this number in all the boxes.

Count in ☐ s along the number track around the edge of this sheet. Using two different coloured crayons, shade each section alternately.

☐ + ☐ = 2 x ☐ = ___

☐ + ☐ + ☐ + ☐ = ___ x ☐ = ___

☐ + ☐ + ☐ + ☐ + ☐ + ☐ = ___ x ☐ = ___

☐ + ☐ + ☐ + ☐ + ☐ + ☐ + ☐ + ☐ = ___ x ☐ = ___

10 lots of ☐ = ___ x ☐ = ___   12 lots of ☐ = ___ x ☐ = ___

5 x ☐ = ___
10 x ☐ = ___
20 x ☐ = ___
30 x ☐ = ___
40 x ☐ = ___
50 x ☐ = ___
60 x ☐ = ___
70 x ☐ = ___
80 x ☐ = ___
90 x ☐ = ___
100 x ☐ = ___

Draw ☐ caterpillars each with ☐ legs.

How many legs all together? ☐ x ☐ = ___

Special Assignment 1, see page 74

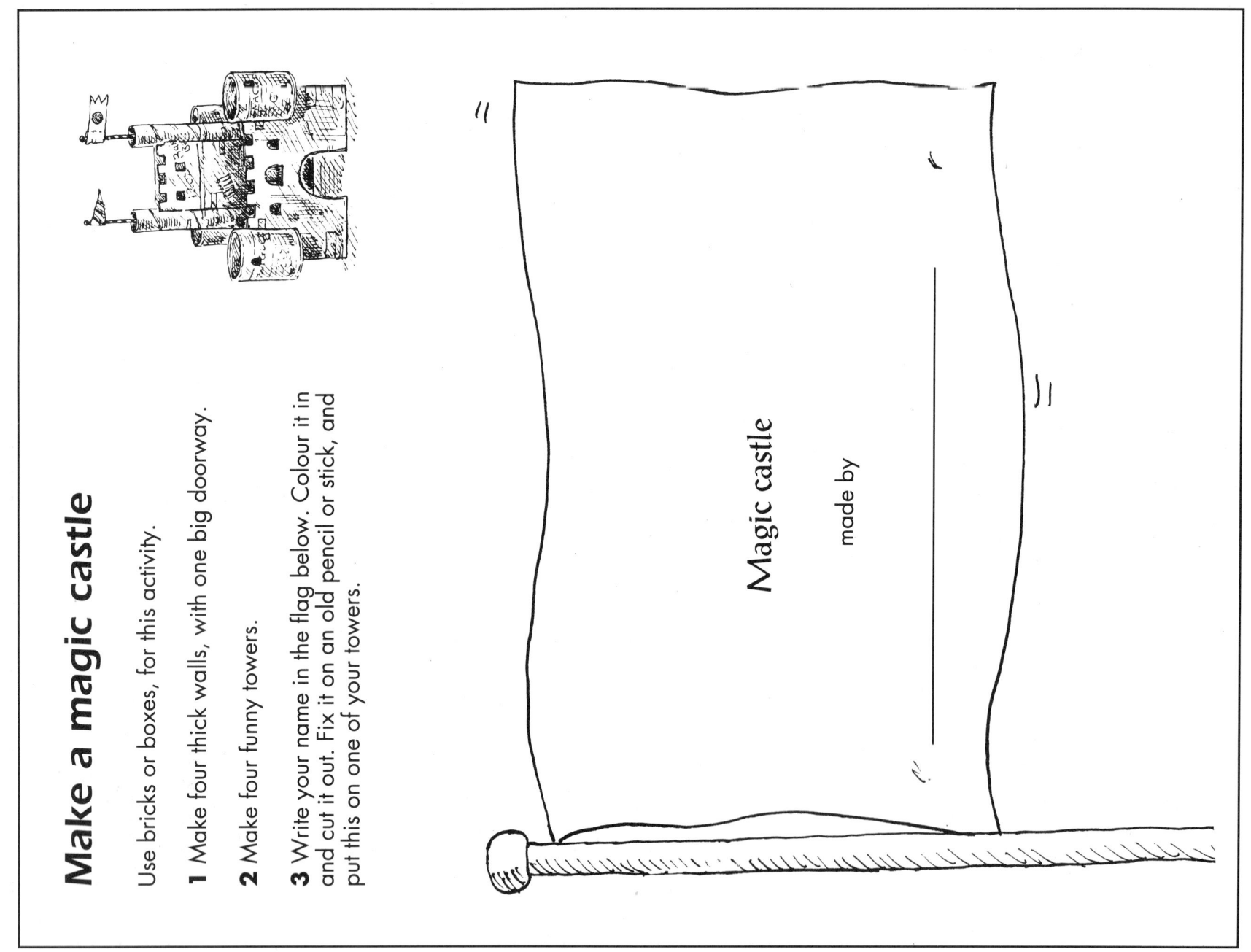

Make a magic castle

Use bricks or boxes, for this activity.

1 Make four thick walls, with one big doorway.

2 Make four funny towers.

3 Write your name in the flag below. Colour it in and cut it out. Fix it on an old pencil or stick, and put this on one of your towers.

Magic castle

made by _____

This page may be copied for use in the classroom and should not be declared in any return in respect of any photocopying licence.

Special Assignment 2, see page 75

Sort six counters

- See how many patterns you can make with just six counters and draw them below.

Sorted by _____

On _____

This page may be copied for use in the classroom and should not be declared in any return in respect of any photocopying licence.

Special Assignment 3, see page 76

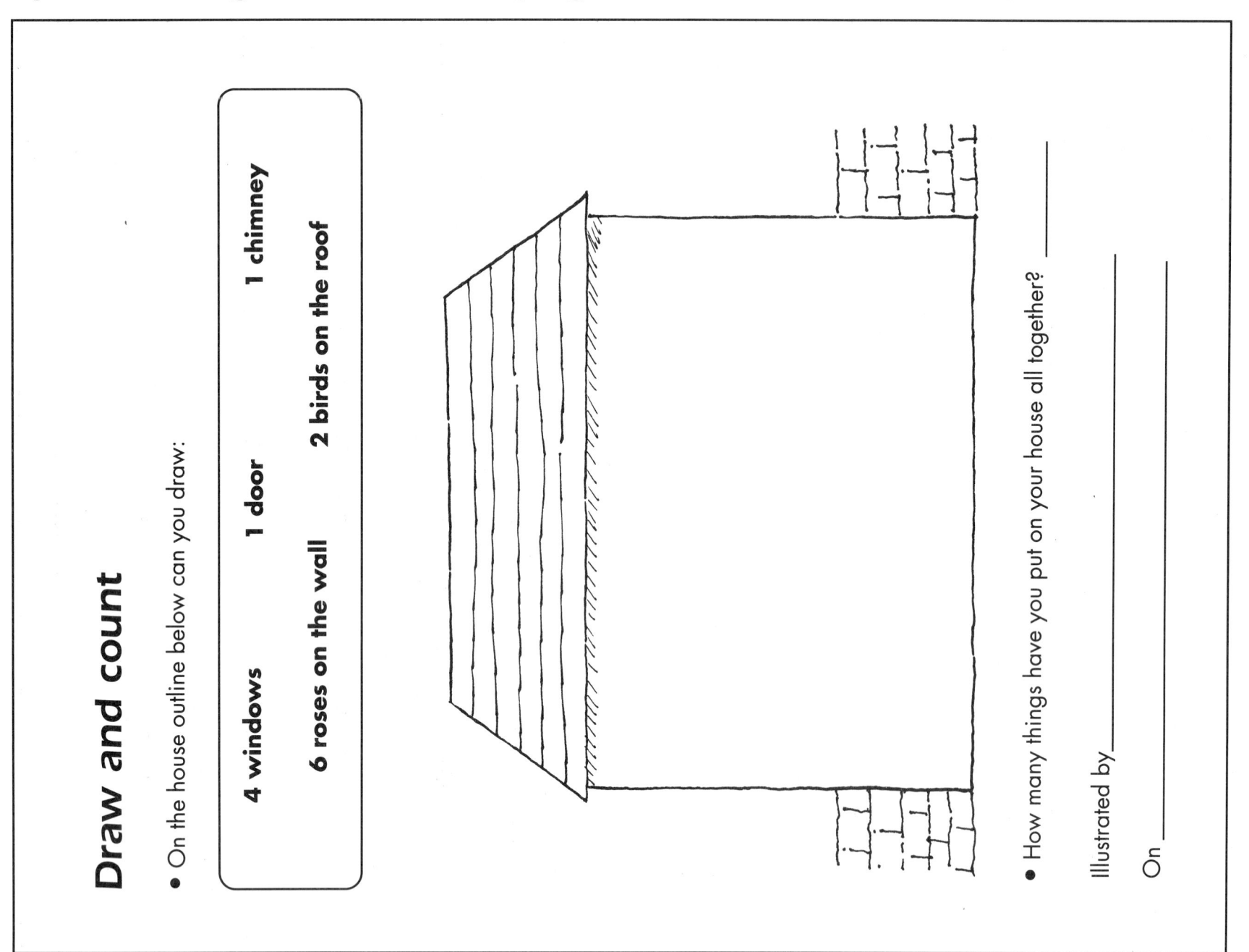

Draw and count

- On the house outline below can you draw:

  | 4 windows | 1 door | 1 chimney |
  | 6 roses on the wall | | 2 birds on the roof |

- How many things have you put on your house all together? _____

Illustrated by _____

On _____

This page may be copied for use in the classroom and should not be declared in any return in respect of any photocopying licence.

Special Assignment 4, see page 77

Invent a new toy or game

- Use corks, pins, thread, paper-clips and card.

See what you can invent! Draw your invention in the space below.

- Write about your invention on the label below. Cut it out, fold it and put it by the new toy.

Fold along the dotted line and place this by the invention.

This new toy is _____

It was invented by _____

on _____

Special Assignment 5, see page 78

Spell the magic

- Fill this magic square with letters to spell as many words as you can. Each of your words must contain at least one of the letters written already.

	a	b	r	a	c	a	d	a	b	r	a
b											
r						r					r
a				b				b			b
c				a				a			a
a				d				d			d
d	a	b	r	a	c	a	d	a	b	r	a
a						c					c
b						a					a
r						r					r
a		b				b					b
a	b	r	a	c	a	d	a	b	r	a	

Spelled by _____

On _____

Special Assignment 6, see page 79

Research about parrots

- Go the library and find a book or encyclopaedia with pictures and information about parrots to record here.

Other kinds of parrots:
_____
_____
_____

What they eat:
_____
_____

Did you know that:
_____
_____
_____
_____

Researched by: _____
On: _____

This is a drawing of a .... parrot

This page may be copied for use in the classroom and should not be declared in any return in respect of any photocopying licence.

Special Assignment 7, see page 80

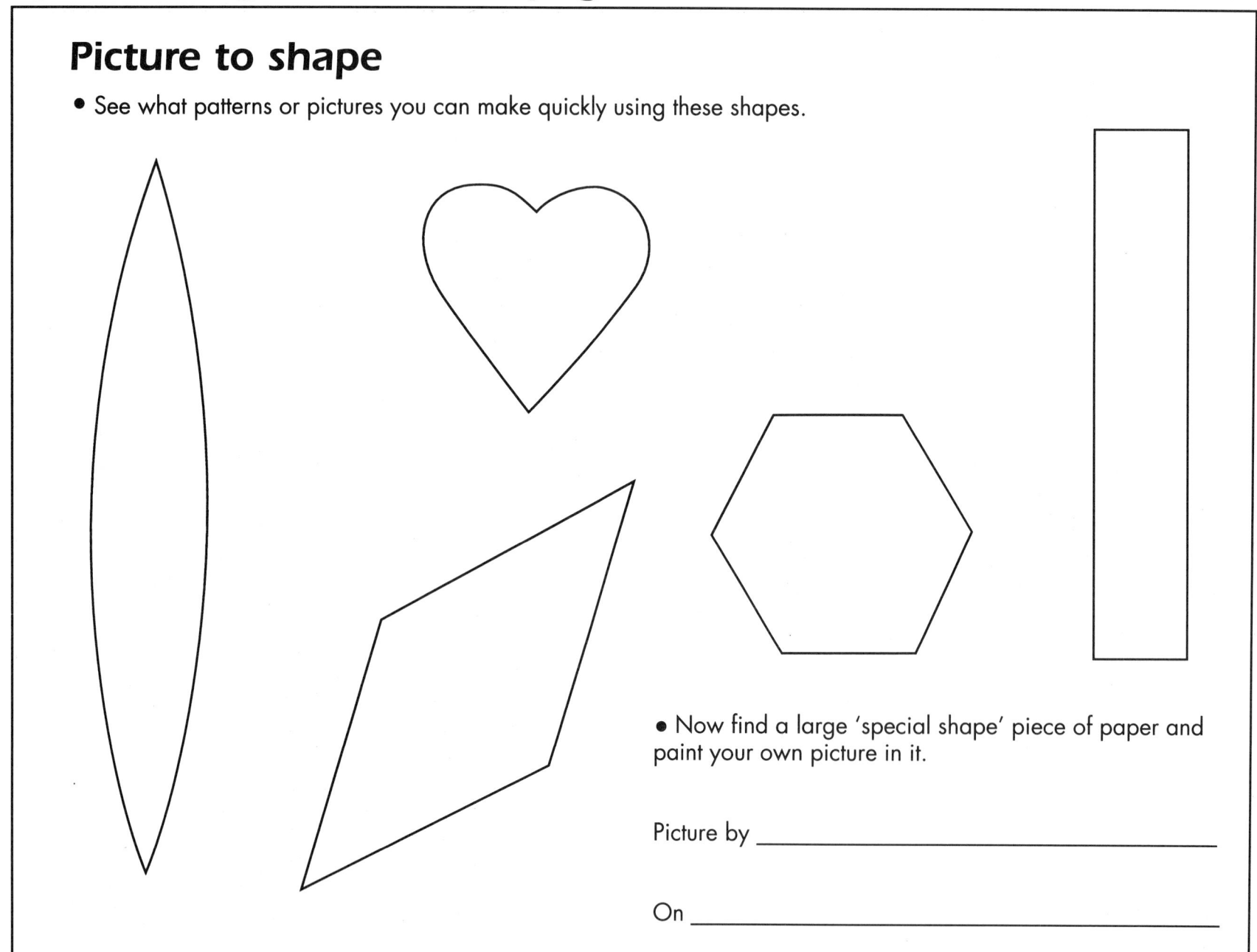

Picture to shape

- See what patterns or pictures you can make quickly using these shapes.

- Now find a large 'special shape' piece of paper and paint your own picture in it.

Picture by _____

On _____

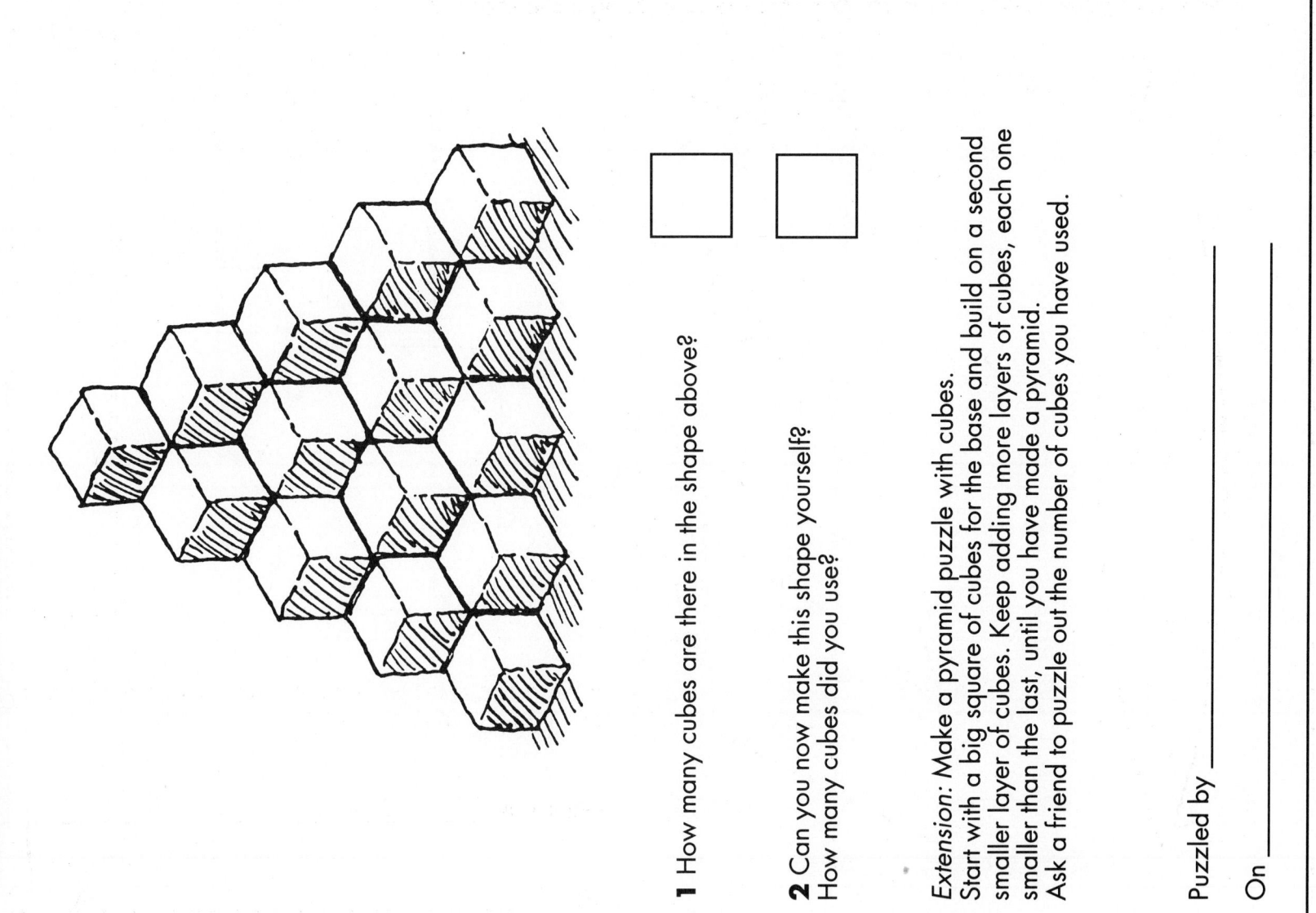

Special Assignment 8, see page 81

Puzzle with cubes

1 How many cubes are there in the shape above?

☐ ☐

2 Can you now make this shape yourself?
How many cubes did you use?

Extension: Make a pyramid puzzle with cubes.
Start with a big square of cubes for the base and build on a second smaller layer of cubes. Keep adding more layers of cubes, each one smaller than the last, until you have made a pyramid.
Ask a friend to puzzle out the number of cubes you have used.

Puzzled by _____

On _____

This page may be copied for use in the classroom and should not be declared in any return in respect of any photocopying licence.

Special Assignment 9, see page 82

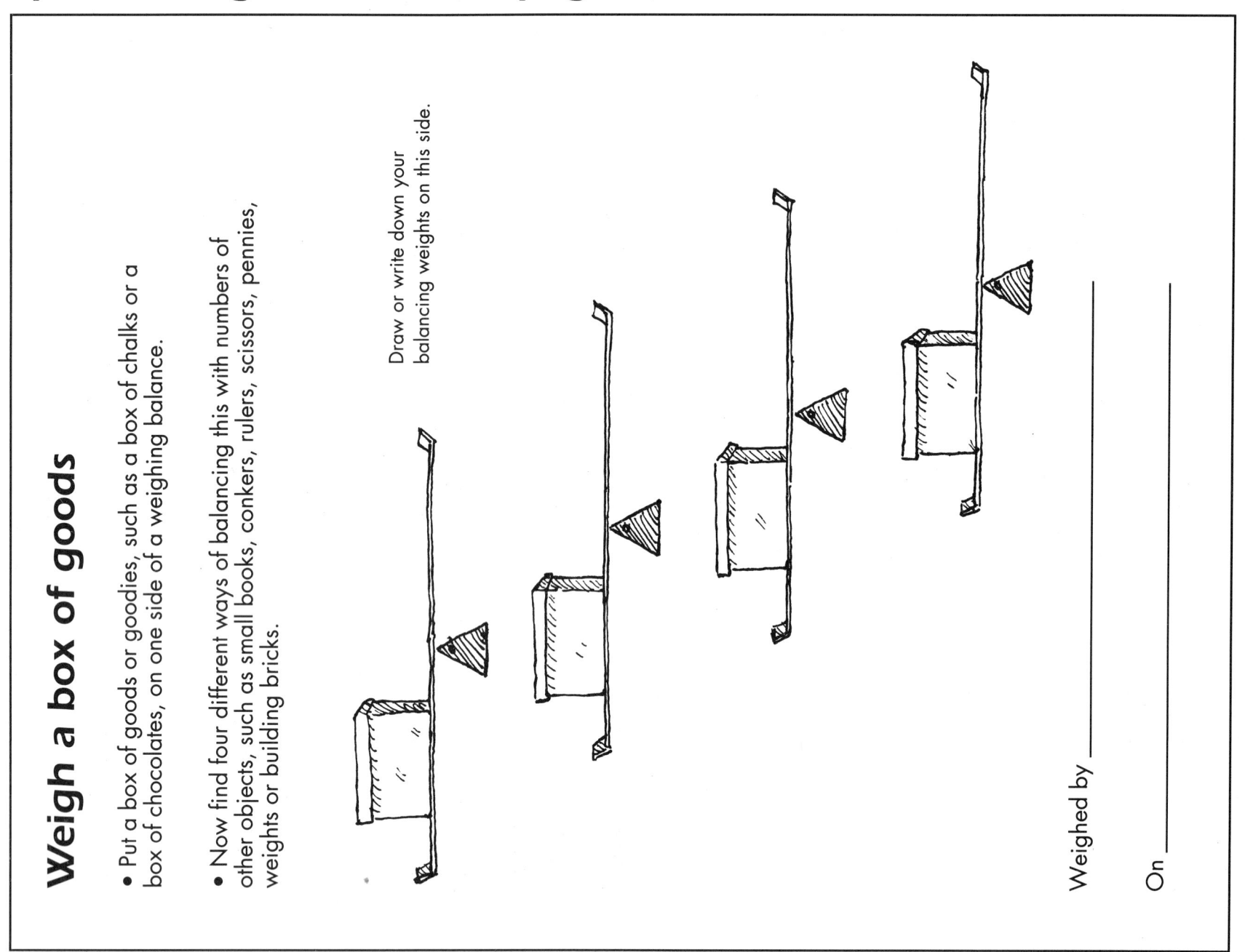

Weigh a box of goods

- Put a box of goods or goodies, such as a box of chalks or a box of chocolates, on one side of a weighing balance.

- Now find four different ways of balancing this with numbers of other objects, such as small books, conkers, rulers, scissors, pennies, weights or building bricks.

Draw or write down your balancing weights on this side.

Weighed by _____

On _____

This page may be copied for use in the classroom and should not be declared in any return in respect of any photocopying licence.

Special Assignment 10, see page 83

Imagine you're a mouse!

Imagine you are a mouse.

Draw a picture of how you look in the space below.

Where do you live? _____

What do you like to eat? _____

What adventures have you had? _____

Who are you really? _____

Special Assignment 11, see page 84

Observe and draw

- Look at somebody working and try to draw what you see.

Drawing of _____
Observed by _____
On _____

This page may be copied for use in the classroom and should not be declared in any return in respect of any photocopying licence.

Special Assignment 12 – Test with a magnet, see page 85

- Find six things that a magnet 'pulls'.

- Write down their names below and put ✓ ✓ (two ticks) for a strong pull and ✓ for a weak pull.

1 _____

2 _____

3 _____

4 _____

5 _____

6 _____

- What do you notice about the things with two ✓s?

_____

_____

_____

_____

Tested by _____

On _____

This page may be copied for use in the classroom and should not be declared in any return in respect of any photocopying licence.

Special Assignment 13, see page 86

Calculate number rows

- Use a calculator to add these rows of numbers:

1+2+3+4+5+6+7+8+9+10= ☐

11+12+13+14+15+16+17+18+19+20= ☐

21+22+23+24+25+26+27+28+29+30= ☐

- Look at your totals so far and see if you can add the following rows more quickly without the calculator.

31+32+33+34+35+36+37+38+39+40 = ☐

41+42+43+44+45+46+47+48+49+50 = ☐

51+52+53+54+55+56+57+58+59+60 = ☐

61+62+63+64+65+66+67+68+69+70 = ☐

71+72+73+74+75+76+77+78+79+80 = ☐

81+82+83+84+85+86+87+88+89+90= ☐

- Are you sure you are right? If not, check with the calculator again.

Calculated by _____

On _____

Special Assignment 14 – Measure the distance, see page 87

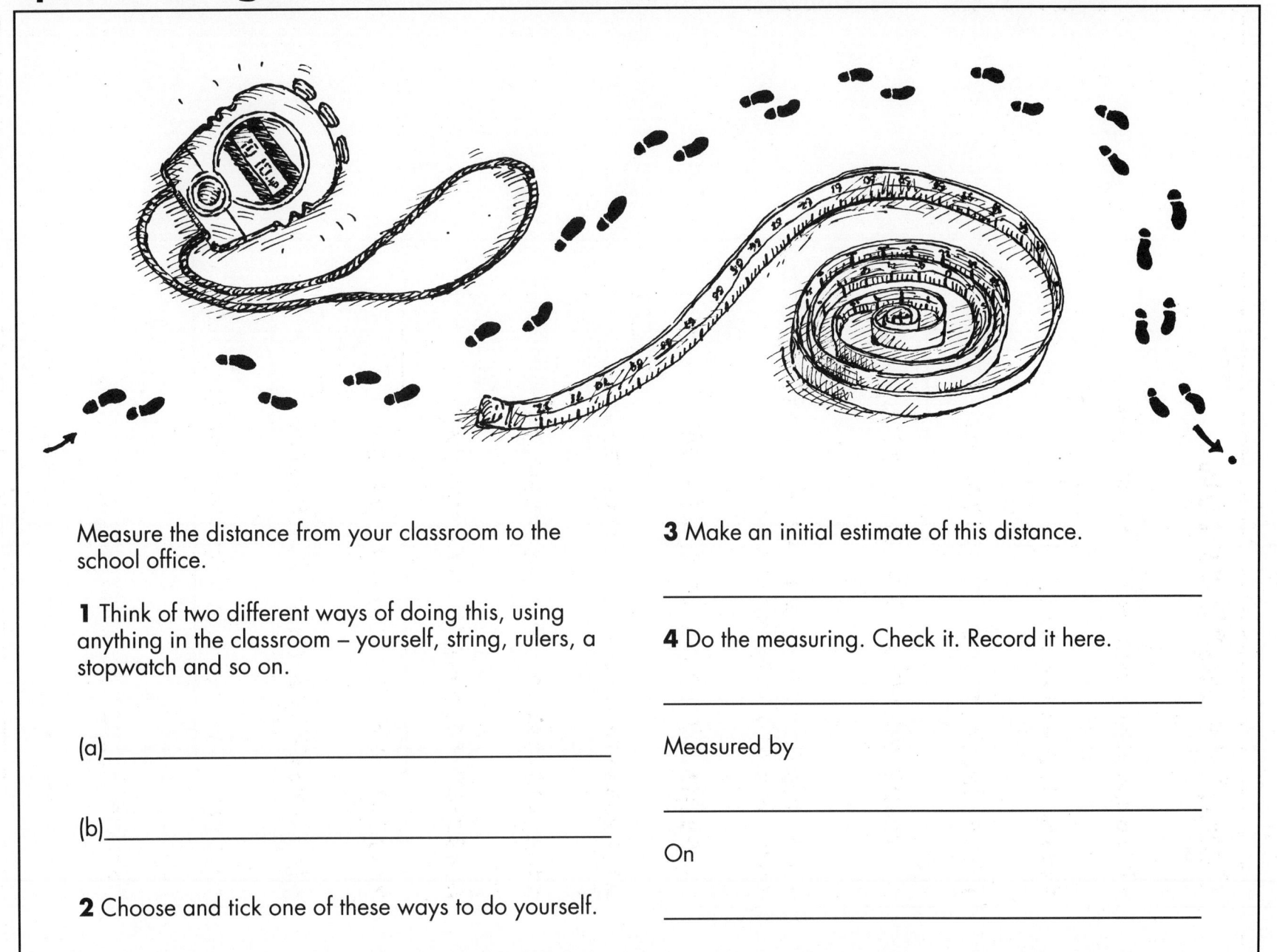

Measure the distance from your classroom to the school office.

1 Think of two different ways of doing this, using anything in the classroom – yourself, string, rulers, a stopwatch and so on.

(a) _____

(b) _____

2 Choose and tick one of these ways to do yourself.

3 Make an initial estimate of this distance.

_____

4 Do the measuring. Check it. Record it here.

_____

Measured by

_____

On

_____

This page may be copied for use in the classroom and should not be declared in any return in respect of any photocopying licence.

Special Assignment 15, see page 88

Question and quiz

- Can you think of and then write down five questions which all have the same answer? This might be your name, a name of another person, animal, place ... It could be anything!

1. _____ ?

2. _____ ?

3. _____ ?

4. _____ ?

5. _____ ?

Answer _____

Questions by _____

On _____

This page may be copied for use in the classroom and should not be declared in any return in respect of any photocopying licence.

Special Assignment 16, see page 89

Process a story

1 On a word processor, type in the words of a typical story beginning like:

Once upon a time...

2 Set the scene for a strange and exciting story – something like:

...there were three wild pigs. They made terrible noises and they told terrible tales.

3 Then make one of the characters decide to tell a story:

...One dark night Little Pig said to Big Pig 'Tell me a story.' So she began.

4 Now use the COPY and PASTE keys to write this story again. Ask someone to help you if you are unsure about this. Copy the story again and again.

5 Print out your story. See if you can cut out the different parts and put them in a circle to make them everlasting.

This page may be copied for use in the classroom and should not be declared in any return in respect of any photocopying licence.

Special Assignment 17, see page 90

Listen in

- Sit in your place and listen for a while to any talking that may be going on around you. Then list some of the odd remarks, words or noises that catch your ears – especially ones that are repeated. Can you make this into a poem? Write your poem below.

Listening in

Listened by _____

On _____

This page may be copied for use in the classroom and should not be declared in any return in respect of any photocopying licence.

Special Assignment 18, see page 91

Weather report

Date _____

Time _____

Amount of cloud cover

_____

Position of sun (if visible)

_____

Temperature by outside door

_____

Any signs of rain

_____

Wind conditions

_____

Visibility

_____

General comment

_____

Reported by

_____

This page may be copied for use in the classroom and should not be declared in any return in respect of any photocopying licence.

Two minute tasks, see page 92

A very short story — See if you can write a full story in two lines.	*A fancy face* — Draw a face with as many features as you can put on it.	*Learn two lines* — Read a poem and see if you can memorise at least the first two lines.	*Bird watching* — Go to the window and see how many birds you can see and identify.	*Dream away* — Sit back and just dream of being somewhere far, far away.	*Tidy your desk*
Speed read — Set the timer and see how many words you can read.	*One minute time test* — Count slowly up to 60 and see how close this is to one minute on the clock. Then do it once more to see if your timing is more accurate.	*Clock watching* — Do nothing but look at the clock for two whole minutes. Does the time seem to pass slowly or quickly.	*Speed writing* — Set the timer and see how many words you can write.	*A noise count* — Set the timer, then listen to and count how many different noises you can hear.	*Pet or plant check* — Check to see whether the classroom pet or plant needs any water or other attention.

This page may be copied for use in the classroom and should not be declared in any return in respect of any photocopying licence.

Ten minute tasks, see page 92

Win a million Double 1, double 2 and keep on doubling your answer until you reach a seven-figure number (1,048,576)	*Make an improvement* Go to one of the special interest areas of your classroom and do something to improve it and also improve your own knowledge.	*Do a good deed* Think of small job that needs to be done in the classroom and then do it quietly without disturbing anybody.	*Spell check* Look through some of your recent writing and make a list of five words which you had trouble spelling. Check these out and test yourself again.	*Learn a poem* Find a short poem and see if you can learn it by heart.	*Make your own words* See how many words you can make out of the letters of your name.
Read and read and read See how many pages of a book you can read.	*Think ahead* Make a list of things that you will be or should be doing next.	*Think of something else* Write a list of things that you would rather be doing just now.	*Sketch* Do a drawing of your teacher.	*Doodle* Draw a funny shape and fill in all the space in and around it with patterns.	*Just think* Write down every thought that comes into your head during this time.

This page may be copied for use in the classroom and should not be declared in any return in respect of any photocopying licence.

Other titles in this series

A Green School
Art
Assemblies
Calculator Activities
Christmas Activities
Christmas Art and Craft
Classroom Management
Computer Activities
Dance and Movement
Design and Technology
Display
Drama
Easter Activities
English
Environmental Studies
Festivals
Games for PE

Geography
Geography Projects
History
History Projects
Imaginative Writing
Indoor and Outdoor Games
Language Development
Language Skill
Lifesavers
Maths Activities
Maths Games
Maths Projects
Media Education
More Christmas Art and Craft
Music
The Outdoor Classroom
Poetry

Problem Solving
Reading Activities
Responses to Music
Science
Science Fun
Seasonal Activities
Spelling
Summer Activities
Supply Teaching
Time Management
Timesavers
Using Books in the Classroom
Word Games
World of Work
Writing